BREAKING THE BOUNDARIES

Jorik Mol

BREAKING THE BOUNDARIES

On Lived-Experience Mentorship for Autistic Students in Higher Education

Disability Studies
Collection Editor
Damian Mellifont

This book is dedicated to everyone who has had a Jorik, will be a Jorik, or has always needed a Jorik and never had one.

First published in 2025 by Lived Places Publishing

All rights reserved. No part of this publication may be reproduced, stored in a retrieval system, or transmitted in any form or by any means, electronic, mechanical, photocopying, recording, or otherwise, without prior permission in writing from the publisher.

No part of this book may be used or reproduced in any manner for the purpose of training artificial intelligence technologies or systems. In accordance with Article 4(3) of the Digital Single Market Directive 2019/790, Lived Places Publishing expressly reserves this work from the text and data mining exception.

The author and editor have made every effort to ensure the accuracy of the information contained in this publication but assume no responsibility for any errors, inaccuracies, inconsistencies, or omissions. Likewise, every effort has been made to contact copyright holders. If any copyright material has been reproduced unwittingly and without permission, the publisher will gladly receive information enabling them to rectify any error or omission in subsequent editions.

Copyright © 2025 Lived Places Publishing

British Library Cataloguing in Publication Data
A CIP record for this book is available from the British Library.

ISBN: 9781916704619 (pbk)
ISBN: 9781916704633 (ePDF)
ISBN: 9781916704626 (ePUB)

The right of Jorik Mol to be identified as the Author of this work has been asserted by them in accordance with the Copyright, Design and Patents Act 1988.

Cover design by Fiachra McCarthy
Book design by Rachel Trolove of Twin Trail Design
Typeset by Newgen Publishing, UK

Lived Places Publishing
P.O. Box 1845
47 Echo Avenue
Miller Place, NY 11764

www.livedplacespublishing.com

Acknowledgements

This book came about in the oddest way possible. I want to thank Michael Boezi, David Parker and Cindy Durand for finding me and taking a chance on a still-unpublished autistic writer without a PhD or an academic position. Thanks also to Lynda at Jessica Kingsley Publishing for allowing me the time and space to create something that is impossible to extricate from the work I am doing with her. I want to thank my employers, specifically Joe Barton and Amanda Holt, for their patience and interest in this work. Thanks to all the actually autistic mentors I've met since signing this contract, especially Rachel Griffiths. Thanks to Brian Irvine for vital conversations, since 2023. We're going to continue having those, I hope. Thanks to Nick Newby, my PA, Sara-Louise Ackrill and everyone else at Wired Differently. Thanks to Max Bastow for vital editorial support, and so, so much more. Thanks to my friends, family and especially my partner, Luke. I love you more than oxygen – and as an asthmatic, you'll get how much I love breathing! Thanks for putting up with me and my neuroses and unfurling into the greatest human being I will ever know. Thanks to Damian Mellifont, whose calls I look forward to, even if the time difference means I have to get up very early indeed. Thanks also to Malini Harikumar and John Britto Stephen for their work editing this book. I'm sorry for being such a nightmare about quotation marks. Most of all, thank you to all my mentees, none of whom I name here, but all of whom have given feedback on the chapters that concern our working relationship. I am so proud of the people you have become and will one day be still. Thank you for taking me on your journeys, if only for a while.

Abstract

Universities can sometimes exclude Autistic students from getting the most out of their experience. As one of the few Actually Autistic Higher Education mentors for Autistic students in the UK, Jorik Mol seeks to improve the educational experience of neurodivergent students by encouraging breaking boundaries, challenging the system and providing places where students can be themselves.

Drawing from his own lived experience, and with stories from his own mentees, Mol offers guidance on how to best support students, emphasising the need to teach radical empathy, values-driven motivation, and self-advocacy.

Exploring topics including community, boundaries, and burnout, while pushing hard against the status quo, this book is ideal reading for students of Education, Disability Studies, Sociology, Psychology, and Queer and LGBT+ Studies, as well as education practitioners and policymakers, autistic people, and allies who want to be part of a movement for neuroqueer liberation within the education sector.

Key words

Disability; neurodiversity; University; DEIB; empathy; values-driven motivation; self-advocacy; communities; boundaries; burnout; autism; neuroqueerness; friendship; work-life balance; LGBTQIA+; gender; sexuality; race and ethnicity; class; activism

Preface

This book is based on my practice as a community organiser and autistic professional. I operate from the social model of disability, understanding barriers to disabled people to be socially and politically expedient for the majoritarian group in society. Therefore, my practice includes supporting those who have not (yet) been diagnosed as autistic. Likewise, I consider the terms 'autism', 'ADHD' and other diagnostic terms to be historically contingent and created from deficit-frames based on an imaginary behavioural norm at a specific historical moment, for specific historical purposes, influenced by Edward Said and his book **Orientalism**.

I am deeply influenced by Damian Milton's Double Empathy Problem, a basic understanding of which I take as read in this book. In my other book, **Feeling Fast and Slow**, I put the Double Empathy Problem to work, analysing the iniquities faced by autistic people versus our neurotypical peers. This I call 'neurochauvinism': the mainstream idea that there's only one way to have a brain, and whatever that way is, it's not ours.

Furthermore, I take the 'neurodiversity paradigm' as a given, as well as understanding the challenges faced by non-white, queer and otherwise disabled autistics to access community and healthcare in a way that matches their needs.

I am committed not just to equality of opportunity (which is usually a weasel word for upholding existing iniquities in society) but to equality of outcomes. This will hopefully explain my somewhat idiosyncratic view of higher education.

The term 'neuroqueer' originates with Nick Walker, and I have found it increasingly useful in understanding what being autistic actually means to autistic people. We are 'queered' by the way our brains are distinct from those around us. That 'queering' is a Butlerian concept, but basically, it means that our society positions us in certain roles, due to characteristics we already possess. In the case of neuroqueers, as I understand it, this makes us distinct from our peers in specific, socially constructed ways. To be neuroqueer is to be 'disabled' socially, due to our identities essentially being constructed around us, from the outside in, to be a certain **kind of person**.

Lastly, I am an activist against conversion therapy, which includes its brand names ABA, PBS, Teamteach and TEACCH. These systems intend to make us 'indistinguishable from our peers', according to their originator, Ole Ivar Lovaas, who, after inventing ABA, used it as a basis to create modern conversion therapy for queer people, which is now freely available on the open market. I take it as read that ABA is conversion therapy, since conversion therapy is the direct consequence of ABA.

Contents

Warning		xi
About the author		xii
Introduction		xiii
Learning objectives		xvii
Chapter 1	Jorik	1
Chapter 2	Adam	17
Chapter 3	Marcus	29
Chapter 4	Brandon	39
Chapter 5	Miles	45
Chapter 6	Lissa	49
Chapter 7	Esther	61
Chapter 8	Daisy	69
Chapter 9	Zoey	81
Chapter 10	Stephen	91
Chapter 11	Nik	101
Chapter 12	Noah	109
Chapter 13	Tim	115
Chapter 14	Jack	121
Chapter 15	Emma	125
Chapter 16	Questions and answers	129

Conclusion 153

Recommended projects/assignments/discussion questions 156

References 157

Recommended further reading 158

Index 159

Warning

This book contains explicit references to, and descriptions of, situations which may cause distress. This includes references to and descriptions of:

- Suicidal thoughts, intentions, and actions
- Psychotic delusions and hallucinations
- Violent assault

  - Ableism, discrimination, and microaggressions
  - Homophobia, biphobia, transphobia and acephobia
  - Sexual violence and misogyny
  - Eugenics, racism and systemic abuse
  - Trauma and PTSD
  - Frequent use of strong language throughout

References to potentially distressing topics occur frequently and throughout the book. Lastly, Jorik is a very opinionated activist. The views expressed in this work do not necessarily represent the views of Lived Places Publishing Ltd., or of the autistic community in general or of wider liberation movements.

About the author

Jorik Mol (he/him) is an autistic mentor, advocate, educator, writer and community organiser. Born in the Netherlands, Jorik moved to the United Kingdom in 2010, settling permanently in 2013. Qualifying as a teacher in 2017, Jorik has been an autistic mentor since 2021, the practice of which is the subject of this book. In addition, Jorik runs the QND Network, a queer neurodivergent writers' group, which creates a space for neuroqueer writers to connect, create and collaborate. He also runs the Autistic Wellbeing Group at Bath Spa University. He has spoken at Oxford University, the Association of University Presses (2021) and Autscape (2023), as well as providing training and consultancy to businesses, schools and other organisations on inclusion and equity for neurodivergent people in wider society. On his website, Jorik writes a regular blog, which you can find at: https://www.jorikmol.com. Besides all this, Jorik writes autistic fiction, aims to create neurodivergent theatre, and aims to neuroqueer research. Together with his autistic fiancé, Luke, dozens of cuddly toys, and hundreds of books, Jorik lives in Bath, UK.

Introduction

I kind of fell into being an autistic advocate. It wasn't something I sought out, but I was, rather, picked. This makes it sound like an Oprah Winfrey moment: "and *you* get a cause, and *you* get a cause, and *you* get a cause…" It really wasn't as fancy as that, though utterly, utterly life-changing. I was at an Autism Oxford event in early 2018, purportedly doing some 'continued professional development' (which is how I explained it to my line manager at the school I was teaching for), but really doing research for my own autistic novel I had started 18 months before. That book had already changed my life before I'd even finished it, allowing me to think of myself as part of a wider movement, pretty much for the first time. I never thought I had a community, especially since I had a track record of failed attempts to find one, best described by US comedian Maria Bamford as 'the Burning Bridges Tour'. I met the man who is now my partner and a significant number of people committed to what I was trying to do.

A few weeks before this conference, I left a form of therapy I'd been expected to complete, consequent to a misdiagnosis of personality disorder. In this NHS group therapy course, we were expected to mentalise. Now, mentalisation is a psychological term for gaining an awareness of the feelings we are feeling and the sensations our bodies undergo. This course had a different view of mentalisation: if you experience overwhelming emotions, you need to stop yourself, figure out what you're feeling, assess the emotion, change it, and go on your merry way. Yeah, we were supposed to modify our emotions at will. Obviously, autistic meltdowns occur because of a surfeit of emotions and sensory information; that's why they're meltdowns – they're a loss of control. When I pointed that out to the therapist, he started shouting at me. I have a talent for making people show their true colours around me, which is a blessing and a curse.

The speaker at the conference was Tony Attwood, a well-known British-Australian researcher and practitioner on autism spectrum conditions. Like other non-autistic researchers in the autism field who have been around for a long time, he is not uncontroversial or unproblematic, but he's never not been kind to me. This is where his kindness started. When I asked my question about this therapeutic barrier imposed on autistic people, he was actually a bit upset on my behalf and said that I should never have had to experience this. Quite accidentally – or not – a member of staff from a nearby NHS trust left me a message, if I was interested in coming in for a conversation. That conversation turned into a job, which turned into running an autistic experience group, which I did alongside being a teacher and a personal tutor. I worked there until early 2020, when Covid and national politics came together to stamp out the group and our plans to improve autistic people's lives. I made a lot of friends through my work and connected with a tonne of autistic activists, who all encouraged me to keep going. If you do not like what you read in this book, blame them. I jest of course: anything in this book is me, as a mentor, thinking through my own practice, making a few jokes, and allowing you to connect with this work, how it has revolutionary potential and what it says about the way autistic people can find connections and self-organisation.

This book is not going to rehash what you should already know about autism. Yes, we may show certain behaviours, like selective mutism, stimming, hyperfocus on our interests and/or difficulties in processing the sensory world. We can have meltdowns, sensory overloads, shutdowns, stick out like a sore thumb or fade into the background. No, we do have a sense of humour. No, we do have empathy. Yes, we're equally likely to be male or female, from every ethnicity or heritage, with or without learning disabilities. We are, however, a lot more likely to be LGBTQIA+. All that is true, more or less. This book takes that knowledge, in whatever shape it was passed down to you, culturally, as a given. This book is written for actually autistic people who wish to become mentors, who live that experience every day. In it, I show the cases of 14 autistic people I have supported over the past three-and-a-half years to stretch, question and think through what best practice would look like for other autistic people who want to do this particular job. I am highly opinionated and have a very specific outlook on neurodiversity politics, coming at it from a liberation-focused, anti-capitalist perspective. My perspectives on empathy, in particular, are quite the opposite of what is, embarrassingly, *still* the medical mainstream view. I will not go into this, or other theory too deeply, please read *Feeling Fast and Slow* for that. Still, when relevant, I will outline theoretical positions within these case studies, state my perspective and show how my practice is influenced by the values that I bring to this work. As I said to my PA the other week when he asked about how to present me and what I do to the world, I said: "my values are my brand", and was a little bit sick at the back of my mouth. As much as it pained me to say it at the time – so much awkward! – I do believe they are. I do what I do because of my values, which are against the status quo, against capitalist extraction from the lives of queer and disabled people, against the norms of existence that hold us back. Only the very worst autistic people make it big: Elon Musk, for example, richest man in history, whose repellent views on disabled people, women and labour rights are well known (NB: this comment is not necessarily representative of the views of *Lived Places Publishing*).

As for the case studies, they make up the bulk of this book. They are not exhaustive; I still work with many of these young people and some topics we discussed were not relevant for what each case study ended up becoming. All mentees have given feedback on the chapters that pertain to their experiences, and I have adjusted and modified their narratives in accordance with their perspectives. As I do with all parts of my job, I assume that all autistic people are right about their own experience, with caveats. Sometimes, we are clearly acting against our own best interests. I know, I've been there. The final chapter is a series of questions, which I want you to think through. The first chapter, however, is about the biggest case of my career, i.e. me. How did I become a mentor exactly?

Learning objectives

- To explain the socially constructed nature of disability, queerness and neuroqueerness.
- To challenge mainstream perceptions of boundaries while working with neurodivergent students, while remaking those boundaries in collaboration with the students.
- To provide creative feedback on the topic of friendship within a mentor-mentee relationship and show the potential risks involved in this relationship.
- To recognise the distinctions between neurodivergent and neurotypical collaborations, to challenge mainstream perceptions of autistic people, and be mindful of the political basis of neurodivergent rights.
- To become a mentor for other autistic people.

1
Jorik

In 2021, towards the end of our tenancy in Reading, my partner and I decided to move to Bath. I had just started as an independent autistic activist and knew that I was good in this field. I'd recently been let go from a position as an actually autistic so-called 'Expert by Experience' at a local NHS trust. The money was gone, they said. They probably weren't wrong. My experiences, stuck in between NTs of various stripes, having to bridge the gap between neurotypes and systems were not great. Let's say that it started in a complicated way and just became more difficult as time went on. The best parts of my week were the Autism Experience Group, which I ran. There were no neurotypical people present in the room, which was made accessible in collaboration with the attendees, who were – as I insisted – paid for their time. These meetings were amazing. I was so impressed with everyone. We really made a difference, too.

However, I found that there were very severe problems, mostly to do with the people who were otherwise in charge. It was difficult to challenge the overriding sense that I was an unwelcome guest, who disagreed strongly with the way things were usually done in the system, such as the use of behaviour modification, which I will refer to as conversion therapy practices. For more on ABA and behaviourism, see *Neurotribes* (Silberman, 2015), *Neuroqueer*

Heresies (Walker, 2022) and *Feeling Fast and Slow* (Mol, 2026), as well as my 2023 talk for the University of Exeter, which you can find on my website. These are systems to restrain and retrain autistic people in distress to be more neurotypical – whether that imposition is stated directly or not, we cannot ignore the normative power that systems like ABA, PBS (ABA's passive-aggressive, *very British* cousin), Teamteach (restraint, like the kind used against Elijah McClain and George Floyd) and TEACCH (a system that uses common sense communication tools, so is not explicitly harmful, but it is still wildly expensive and funds conversion therapy practices in other ways) were performing upon the bodies of autistic people. When I challenged my colleague on their support for ABA, I was called anti-scientific. When I retorted that science is done by people and for particular political ends, my colleague told me the conversation was over. I have plenty more stories, but knowing that NHS trusts are happy to litigate against disabled people, I will not tell them here. You will find more stories in the dissertation of my friend Jo Minchin, member of the National Autistic Taskforce (Minchin, 2020). I asked Jo how she was getting on with the transcription of my interview. She said: "I'm getting on great! It's been a three fucks and a cunt day." I am a very sweary boy when I'm upset.

So it's 2021. I started as an independent activist and educator. I began doing talks when I was asked to, and I started making connections in the local area – first Oxford, then Reading. Now I was moving to Bath, and I needed to get started there. I found an advertisement for Specialist Mentor – Autism, funded not by the student personally but by Disability Student Allowance. This is a grant, from the Department for Education, that allows disabled students to access higher education in a more equal way than they otherwise would have. For a successful interview, I needed to show teaching qualifications and commitment to autistic people's welfare. I have a CELTA, which allows me to teach English as a Foreign Language, as well as having taken courses on being a teaching assistant during the pandemic, spending more time challenging the course leader than listening, to be honest. He seemed to appreciate it though! For the commitment part, I could show my work in the NHS, my website and my other connections which showed my profile was on the rise. I contacted local Bath-based universities. Both told me they worked with a large corporation that was responsible for the allocation of students for DSA-funded mentoring. I contacted this corporation. Since we were still mid-pandemic (arguably we still are!) and they were really struggling for staff, I got in with relative ease. Even I didn't doubt that I would be fit for this particular job. And I doubt everything! Not even Descartes can out-doubt me. Why didn't I get nervous? Because of all the jobs I'd done, working closely with autistic people has been the thing I felt most naturally talented at. It was easy; it was fun. I was able to exist, as myself, and do what I'm good at: providing reassurance, dealing with potential conflict situations and breaking down barriers for others by advocating. I would be doing what I ended up doing quite naturally within the Experience Group. I would organise people, listen to their concerns and seek to resolve painful situations. I would advocate for them, when systems and individuals had done them harm. I would connect with others, increasing our network of autistic people, who were all, increasingly, proud to be autistic. My greatest memories of this time include creating the first Autistic Pride Oxford, in 2019, as well as representing my local trust at the Oxford Pride 2019, Autistic UK, Autistica and Autscape conferences. As someone who essentially fell ass-backwards into activism, I appeared to suddenly possess skills for organising people around me, and my specific set of values. When I left the NHS Trust, my community was clear: you need to continue doing this. So I did. Being a mentor is nothing if not a natural combination of my work as an activist and as a teacher/tutor.

I start from the perspective that autistic people's experience of the world is correct. That is already a huge job, given that I grew up being told that my brain didn't work right and I wouldn't be able to grasp reality as a consequence. I was pathologised as, well, 'wrong'. I was the kind of person who was wrong about life – that's what the world at least understood about me. My emotional responses, my hyperfixations, my connections with other people and the world around me, my sensory sensitivities, my sense of humour and my talent for languages and imitation: all of that was wrong. Working as an activist, I realised, meant that my increased political awareness grew and I combined my outlook with the work I could actually do in the world. No longer was I someone disabled by being wrong-in-the-world; my empathy and capacity to agitate were fundamental to my politics: as a queer neurodivergent activist. So imagine my shock when the company sent me an online training module that advertised conversion therapy. Things got sweary, I'll tell you that much.

When I got the job, I wouldn't see mentees until September 2021, by which time I would have finished moving to Bath and teaching a course of English for Academic Purposes. First, I had to pay out of pocket for online training created by the National Autistic Society, the UK's most important autism charity, though its audience is, first of all, neurotypical parents of autistic children. I baulked at that, since my training work covers nearly exactly the same ground as those trainings on autism. I enjoyed seeing some of my friends appear in the videos, but I finished them within barely two hours. The next training modules were self-created by the company. Initially, this was nothing I hadn't seen before – mostly old-fashioned terminology, combined with adherence to the now functionally retracted (by its own co-author) Triad of Impairments. Autistic people, to meet the now-discredited diagnosis of Asperger's Syndrome (which I was diagnosed with back in 1996), are deficient in social interaction, social communication and imagination. I am an actual novelist – what the hell you guys?

The Triad of Impairments was created by autism researchers Lorna Wing and Judith Gould. They were only funded to conduct studies on autism if they were to create a brand new diagnostic criterion. Therefore, they created Asperger's Syndrome, named after the then recently deceased Hans Asperger. Anglo-German autism researcher Uta Frith had just translated some of Asperger's work from the 1930s and 1940s, in what turned out to be a highly sympathetic, yet inauthentic portrayal of Asperger's character. In 2018, the American researcher Edith Scheffer wrote *Asperger's Children*, based on archive research she had done on Asperger's role at Spiegelgrund children's hospital in Vienna (Thomson, 2018). In the book, Scheffer, in meticulous detail, smashes Asperger's previous reputation as a kindly 'Oskar Schindler-figure', instead understanding him as a committed Nazi and eugenicist. Eugenics was the apolitical norm across psychiatry and children's healthcare in the first half of the twentieth century. But Asperger was committed not to saving the children he deemed worthy from those who were to be murdered in the T4 destruction programme, but was an active, enthusiastic participant in this system. For Asperger, there was something fascinating about us autistic people, mostly by how far we seemed to pervertedly deviate from the expected norm or *Volksgeist*. Here is where I depart from Scheffer, whose liberal anti-authoritarianism seems to hinge on a fear of otherness in the first place – 'What is the purpose of a diagnosis if we are all the same?' she seems to say, and her autistic son actually says in the afterword. What I find most disturbing instead is the creation of a fascist society based on colonialism, extraction and destruction of those it deems unworthy of lives. That's what I find upsetting about fascism, not the uniforms. I do believe we are fundamentally different from non-autistic people on some as yet impossible-to-define basis to do with our brains, but that this difference is only made a force of exclusion by the choice of the neuro-majority to disempower us.

I base this force on empathy, a ghostly concept that attaches social value judgements to an action as simple as recognising another human being as a human being. Damian Milton (2012) has written extensively on the Double Empathy Problem, where the empathy systems between two groups are meaningfully distinct to such an extent that automatic empathetic responses are not guaranteed across group identities. Instead, each group has to learn to empathise with the other group in a cognitive, controlled manner. That is indeed the goal, but we don't live in a world where those intergroup relations are in any way equal. Instead, autistic people are recognised as highly empathetic within their own group and quite empathetic with non-autistic people, at least within the first second of being exposed to their image and/or voice. Non-autistic people, in turn, are quite naturally empathetic to people who are also non-autistic, but comparatively do not show empathetic responses to autistic people anywhere near to people within their neurotype (Sasson et al., 2017). This has caused a huge discrepancy between autistic people and non-autistics, leaving an empathy gap, where the minoritised group is expected to empathise with the majoritarian one, while that majority neurotype defines the minority as uniquely lacking in empathy. Ouch. I call this cultural self-propelling machine neurochauvinism. As Nick Walker quotes in her book *Neuroqueer Heresies*, "power is to have the ability not to have to learn" (Walker, 135).

Clearly, the creators of these training modules had not had to learn about autism for a very long time. For starters, they looked old. Think mid-2000s. Clearly, they hadn't been updated in years, potentially decades. They were full of advertisements for chemical, nutritional and medical 'cures', strange conspiratorial statements about a lack of vitamin D during pregnancy "causing" autism, wheat-free diets and secretin; a linear "spectrum" of autism from "high-functioning" to "classic, or Kanner's autism", advertisements for ABA and early-intervention conversion "therapies", liberal use of the Autism Speaks puzzle piece logo, deep misgivings of our capacity to be human beings, a pro-treatment attitude that included ABA but also CBT: cognitive behavioural therapy, which many autistics, including myself, have had atrocious experiences with. One of the questions in the test, for which one had to score 95% or more on to pass, was: "Which one of these famous people did NOT have autistic tendencies? Diana Ross, Albert Einstein or Sir Isaac Newton?" Wow. We don't know about Diana Ross, but the subtext is that a Black female artist is always going to be less autistic than two dead white men, one of whom died 300 years ago (the answer was, apparently, Diana Ross). This was not the only example of implicit racism in the module, including an optical illusion that required one to assess whether the person presented was 'an Indian or an Eskimo'. They meant First Nations Americans and Inuit, which are both to be seen in the cartoon. The intention was to allow people to consider 'two ways of looking at things'. Okay, that's fine, I suppose!

My 'favourite' of all the questions was: "Which of these below statements would be unlikely to be said by someone with autism, considering the way they comprehend you, me and I?" "I would like a cup of tea please", "Joe would like a cup of tea", or "Would Jim like to watch TV with David?"

I am still baffled by this question. I really don't know what's expected here. Answer A. implies that we're not supposed to have a sense of self, so we refer to ourselves in the third person. Answer B. implies that other people don't matter to us, so we wouldn't refer to another person having any needs or desires since we're inherently selfish. Answer C. does the same as B again, but the idea is that we wouldn't be polite or be able to speak about third parties, or something, I don't know. And I'm 'a person with autism', according to this training module.

By the way, *never* refer to an autistic person as a 'person with autism' unless they, for their own reasons, request that you do so. If you insist on 'person-first language' that implies you perceive 'autism' as distinct from the person's identity when, in fact, 'I am autistic' is an identity-statement. The entire training module used person-first language like this.

I was, quite literally, shocked and appalled. I got on the phone with the company, which didn't have any autistic people working for them, nor had they ever heard a complaint about these modules. In fact, I later found out that the UK Department for Education – under Conservative leadership since 2010 – had approved these modules in 2020. I tried to raise a complaint with the Disability Student Allowance in 2022, but got nowhere. Since the DfE was run by Conservative Party appointees and the only external oversight body (the Equality and Human Rights Commission) was ruling in favour of allowing conversion therapy for queer people, I did not feel confident that there was anywhere else to go. Meanwhile, I never received full confirmation that the modules were ever meaningfully changed, including the racist language and attitudes, just a verbal assurance that the company would engage with external bodies to make sure that "language" is "up-to-date". Of course, you can use the most inclusive, focus-group-tested language in the world, but if what you're doing is still eugenics, then that doesn't change the outcome one bit.

This. This is how mentors for autistic people are trained, then. Mentors, who have a huge responsibility towards their students, will find them at their most vulnerable in a new environment with huge social and emotional expectations, as well as a shift in what is expected from them academically. As you will see, to be a mentor means to actively push back against the system that causes autistic students to drop out before they finish their degrees and to have a lower quality of life alongside a higher likelihood of traumatic incidents in an environment seemingly *built* to exclude us.

How else are mentors trained? Well, in the majority of cases, prospective mentors have postgraduate certificates in teaching and education. In the UK, these are called PGCEs – Postgraduate Certificates in Education. This means that they are qualified teachers, who may have specialised in special educational needs during their training. Still, SEND is not mandatory for PGCE programmes, so the vast majority will simply not. Ironically, 'behaviour management', and other systems based on cognitive behavioural psychology to punish 'bad' behaviour and reward 'good', IS mandatory for all PGCE candidates. Guess which kids end up in behaviour management classes, or are classed as problems? Yup, it's us, especially if we are also non-white or not native English speakers.

The other way that people qualify to become autism mentors, paid via DSA, is membership of professional organisations, such as the Dyslexia Guild. These are, naturally, expensive members' clubs, which autistic people might not have access to because we are less likely to have the money to buy ourselves in. That is a natural consequence of the shockingly low numbers of autistic people in paid employment in the UK. Plus, when you have difficulties in school because of who you are, fighting to stay afloat in that environment might mean never even getting to university, let alone postgraduate study.

It's important to address the innate difficulties actually autistic people face even getting so-called appropriate qualifications.

I interviewed for a PGCE in Modern Languages, back in 2016. After impressing staff on the course and in my first interview, the head of the course blindsided me, and I was not able to answer a question I did not expect, so I got nervous and had a mini-meltdown. I was cheerfully dismissed, with the reason being that I should work on my mental health. Great. I ended up getting my teaching qualification with the CELTA a year after that, regardless.

A friend of mine did manage to get onto a PGCE course, but he failed the course, because he 'wasn't confident enough in the classroom' to pass – e.g. he was autistic and looked it. Despite the clear ableism in this decision, he has chosen not to fight that particular battle, dealing with the vast student debt he incurred for most of the next couple of decades. So the vast majority of PGCE holders will not themselves be autistic, due to the evident gatekeeping within the education sector. Instead, these graduates will be committed to behaviour management and behaviour modification strategies to increase good (read: neurotypical) and decrease bad (read: not neurotypical) behaviour, without a need to reflect on the basis on which this arbitrary distinction is drawn.

Secondly, mentors may have a Master's degree in Autism. In the UK, a variety of universities offer these degrees, at a very high financial cost to the students themselves. These research or taught degrees differ in their approach, but, until 2015, practically all postgraduate degrees on autism taught some version of behaviour modification 'therapy' as best practice. Only since that time have *some* universities moved to a more neurodiversity-influenced perspective. The majority will still teach ABA. A friend of mine, who completed an ABA course during his psychology degree, said: "It was the most fun module of my entire degree". Of course it is; it has to be. ABA is like Tupperware; there is an ever-increasing, self-created customer base to sell conversion therapy to. Even Damian Milton has to share his faculty with a full-on MSc in ABA and PBS (Accurate from 24/11/2024: Applied Behaviour Analysis and Positive Behaviour Support – MSc – Postgraduate courses – University of Kent). This is shocking, but a compromise that actually autistic people working in academia are forced to make. You will be working alongside people whose practices are actively destroying our communities, whether they intend to do so or not. Because MSc degrees are more accessible to those with the funding and capacity to endure a year or more of high-level training, often in approaches that have very little to do with the actual wellbeing of the people they are supposed to support and using exclusionary testing and marking practices, comparatively few actually autistic people will graduate from these Master's degrees.

Therefore, I was the only actually autistic mentor at the company, a company that has signed exclusivity contracts with a huge number of universities unless students themselves wish not to work with any of the large conglomerates. This bending of the knee to the private sector has been the norm in the health service and education sectors in the UK for decades now, appearing to give choices and options while making it very difficult to choose anything but what the most powerful corporations want.

Being a mentor with lived experience requires you to step outside of the rigid expectations of professionalism. As for me, I'm autistic, so I need to unmask in front of the student, so I don't come across as too detached or as 'just another' support worker. Our relationship is very unique: one-sided but vulnerable. I always say I work for the student, not the other way around. My boundaries are complex: I share a lot of myself, to the benefit of the student. I am open about my own struggles, but I can never be a full friend, which requires reciprocity. I get paid, that's my reward.

I had a mentor, too. I only met her once, back in 2013.

When I was 25, I was not in a good way. I'd been hospitalised in a mental health ward, mostly as punishment for continuing to have autistic meltdowns after starting anti-depressant medication (don't worry, we'll get into the different layers of self-hate when the time comes). The psychiatrists there prescribed me everything but the kitchen sink: 100 mg of Escitalopram, 600 mg of Quetiapine, 4 mg of Clonazepam and 15 mg of Mirtazapine. Because what I really wanted was to be cured of autism and be, in my own words, 'normal'. I know.

Instead of being cured, I just slowed down. I was awake up to 10 hours a day. Meltdowns still happened, I still got conversations and interactions "*wrong*" and I was not normal. I just fell over a lot more. I was on this cocktail for 3.5 years. Much later, I was told that I should have only been on that amount of medication for maybe 2 weeks. No one ever reduced the meds. I do acknowledge that my own attitude to my own behaviour didn't help. I conceived of myself as an animal that needed caging, the drugs being the cage. In short, not a happy bunny. After a year and a half in my self-made holding cell (a haulage container in Amsterdam Zuid-Oost, where such containers were then used as makeshift student flats), I finally graduated.

So, in September of 2013, I moved across the North Sea and started an MA at UCL. Things… didn't start well. I was allocated a mental health mentor, employed by the university. She was probably a very kind, empathetic person. I didn't get to know her well enough to see through the patina of what she was presenting. We met at the UCL refectory, downstairs at its main Bloomsbury campus. It was the first week of October, and I was already burned out.

My main concern? Money. I was surprised at having to pay the full tuition fee at the start of my MA, which did not align with my funding. I needed support in contacting support workers and writing to the right people, but since my medication regime was what it was, I was asleep for about 13–14 hours a day. I didn't have the time to read the allocated books for my courses and take care of myself, let alone do all that admin.

She said the immortal words: "That must be very hard for you."

…Okay…

I must have been perfectly polite to her, because I was raised to be so, but I cannot recall the exact way I reacted through the fog of time and benzos. I also understood that she was being genuine: this was the exact way to show kindness. You express that, while never being able to truly empathise (not living in someone else's head and all), you care and you see how hard it is for that person. Then, you stop.

That's not empathetic; that's a closed door. But it falls within the university's limitations and expectations of boundaries. In fact, she was acting exactly by the book. This **was** an empathetic, caring response, that also, tellingly, allowed the university to sidestep having to take any responsibility. If you don't actually want to support people, this approach is pretty ideal.

Having worked in education and the UK's National Health Service (NHS), I've heard a lot about boundaries, how it's vital to detach oneself from your work and from your own emotions. You are expected to do your job without promising to do anything that takes away from someone else's agency, which is, of course, admirable. We're dealing with people, not dogs.

However, in an age of austerity and cuts, boundaries are used as an excuse to not provide help and support, especially in caring roles. What I needed at the time was someone who didn't just express that she saw how hard it 'must be' for me; I needed someone to take me by the hand and do it with me. I did not have the executive function or capacity to do what I needed to do. I was way too drugged, depressed and overloaded to get anything done.

When she told me that it 'must be so hard' for me, a door shut in my face, but I also immediately lost trust in her as a human being who could potentially help me. Maybe, at a subsequent meeting, she could have been a lot more forthcoming and supportive. I never gave her that chance. The trust was gone.

That's the reason I didn't take up further mentoring support. I wouldn't have been allowed to contact her for support outside of mentoring hours; I would only be allowed to discuss problems 'at' her, without trying to solve them. Reiterating problems, for an autistic person, doesn't solve them. It increases cyclical thinking and served only to rub my nose in how fucked my situation was at that time.

A lot of autistic students do not take up their mentoring support beyond one or two sessions. Why? This attitude, imposed as 'best practice', certainly doesn't help. That's not just incompetence or laziness – an excuse to not actually provide care. Rather, a real lack of interest in what we as neurodivergent people are actually like is at fault here. I speak about that lack of interest and worse as 'neurochauvinism' in *Feeling Fast and Slow* (Mol, 2026). This book is committed to changing that. Boundaries, or what we believe to be boundaries, need reconsidering, reinterpreting and reengaging with, for the benefit of the student. As you will see, each of my case studies shows my complicated engagement with the concept of boundaries. We, as lived-experience mentors, have a very difficult path to tread: between systems of power and the needs of those receiving that power at full force, between our need to support and our need to self-care, the expectations of a student, their family, their university and the department for education. I became aware of that pretty much right away. I saw students barely starting their degrees and already in crisis.

So I could either sit by or do what I do best; make trouble. This book is me making trouble. Let's break some boundaries.

2
Adam

When I meet a new mentee, I always say that I'm autistic, that I'm gay and that my pronouns are he/him, sometimes they/them. I share my access needs: I've probably got Tourette's, and I swear. A lot. I will probably not look them in the eye, either. In short, I will be unmasking in front of that student. I don't expect them to do the same, but neither do I require them to mask their autism for my benefit. I empathise through jokes and humour. I will always try to make someone laugh. I don't hide my own (leftie) politics or the people I share my life with.

When a student has an immediate problem, I am there to help solve it. That's what I do. I will step in and be proactive. Many of them struggle with dyslexia and executive function, so often we start by simply reading the student's emails.

When I started mentoring properly, my first two mentees were at a university local to me. The company I was working with sent me two names and gender identities: one a girl and one a boy. That's it. I sent emails to say hello and book an initial meeting.

The first email I got back was a bit of a shock: the student's name wasn't the girl's name I'd been given, but one they'd changed via deed poll, nor was their changed gender identity handled appropriately – this was not their last name change either. For continuity, let's call him Adam.

I am an autistic activist. I know tonnes of trans and non-binary people, many of whom I am lucky to call my friends. I am just as much an LGBTQIA+ activist as a neurodivergent one. Therefore, I knew my way around this situation. We booked a Zoom meeting where we discussed the name change and the student, accompanied by their mother, told me about their frustration that I was told their deadname rather than their actual name. I said: "I'm sorry I didn't know. Let's get it sorted", and I started drafting an email to the mentoring company, as well as the student's university, which was still using their deadname for their email address.

Importantly, I didn't apologise for the request to get it changed. I took it as a matter of course that name changes could and should be instituted with immediate effect. Had I been more apologetic, we might not have been as successful.

During this first meeting, I was told about the other mentor Adam met the day before me. She had not been transphobic to *them*, but, in a fashion, to me. She'd seen my name and asked: "Gosh what an odd name! Is that a man or a woman?" My student did NOT get a good vibe and has to this date never rebooked a meeting with her. That initial meeting, vital as it is, is all about trust.

By the way, as much of a Gen Z thing as it appears to be, using the word 'vibe' to describe an intuitive sensation, I think it's highly useful. The word 'vibe' expresses the intuitive basis of most of our decision making, an intuition that I personally had learned to distrust. When I was at Sussex University for my study abroad year, I was taking courses in drama in order to put my traumatic experiences at drama school into perspective. I asked a visiting practitioner, a set designer, about her process. She said that she researches deeply and communicates with the other people on the production team but, ultimately, her decisions come from her gut. I said, even though I weighed about 95 kg at the time, "I don't *have* a gut" – or, rather, that my gut instinct was "always wrong". She said: "Wow, okay. I don't think I can help you with that", and she continued clearing up.

When there is no trust at the start of a relationship, we cannot continue. This is because we, as autistic people, learn that we need to be very careful about who we decide to place trust in. Our brains are on the lookout for people who would do us harm. The vast majority of harm inflicted on us, be that physical, emotional or social, is inflicted by those who have good intentions and believe they care for our wellbeing – as the neurotypicals they expect us to be (see *Feeling Fast and Slow*). Therefore, we cannot expect that people will behave empathetically towards us.

As a mentor with lived experience, it's important to let go of neurotypical expectations of communication, which may mean avoiding the spoken word or meeting face-to-face. We might even only meet by exchanging text messages. That's okay: whatever works for the student. As long as you're honest about your own accessibility needs at the start, it's easier for the student to express their own needs. This is stressful, since the student will have become used to ignoring and neglecting their own need for adaptations to normative communication styles.

In their first year, Adam – then using they/them pronouns – was still living with their parents. Adam's mother had spent much of

Adam's life fighting for her child. There had been frequent hospital visits, the horror of engaging with the children's mental health service, also known as CAMHS, and the unending need to advocate. Adam's mother was tired but not done fighting. In me, though, she had found an ally. Unlike other professionals allocated to Adam, I simply asked her child what they wanted me to do, and I would do it. I showed that I was willing to stand up against the university for her child. I saw this as logical. My responsibility is towards the student. I don't care if universities like me – I will still push on. What I care about is the wellbeing of the young person I have a duty of care over. Adam was surprised and, despite their well-founded nervousness, accepted me immediately. I was safe. They needed this – both of them.

Adam had started a degree in creative writing, with which came the need to quantify exactly what the expectations for their creative work would be. I'm a writer too, now writing autistic fiction and running the Queer Neurodivergent Writers' Network, all in English, my second language. I also have an English degree and a Comparative Literature master's. I know my way around words. I've always created worlds and characters, to process the muchness of the universe, to parse reality and to make people laugh. My stories didn't always work, no matter how much effort I put into them. There seemed to be a limited audience for what I did. As a child, I could shrug this off – just another reason people found me weird, I guessed. It wasn't until I sat my exams at 18 and somehow passed an audition for a private drama school that I started facing harsh criticism. What I thought was funny would invariably be taken out of the work I was creating. My insights weren't insightful, my jokes weren't funny, I needed to do: "less! Less! Less!" – so no voices or impressions. I was supposed to be 'authentic', a term that was never explained to me beyond: "I can't tell you what to do, just tell you that what you're doing isn't right." The problem, as the head of my school said, was "not what it is that you're doing that's the problem Jorik, it's *you* doing it". Her intentions were good, too. She just believed I put on a front. Of course I had to: I was closeted and tried to hide my autism, which I needed to, especially since the environments of that drama school were safe for neither disabled nor queer people. It was a horrendous experience, but one I felt I had to undergo because the world wasn't going to change itself for my benefit. I now realise that I was the victim of abuse, no matter the drama school's stated intentions. As a teacher of writing and performance myself, I now know that I am uniquely placed to prevent further distress in the students I was mentoring. Step one: clarity. What did lecturers actually *want* from students? I put that lesson to work with Adam.

After a few emails back and forth, the staff members we spoke to were only able to be vague. Instead, we booked a meeting between me, a leading faculty member, my student and their mum. What we were asking for was clarity; what we got was a lot of awkwardness. The faculty member had clearly not considered disabled and non-neurotypical people in any way as they prepared and administered courses. I remember a long, awkward pause after Adam asked a question, with the member of staff responding with a thousand-yard stare that only said: "help me". After the call, we were finally able to get clarification on what was expected and started preparing for the first assessment. I'm a qualified teacher of English for Academic Purposes, so I was able to help Adam when they ran phrasings and ideas past me.

Writing an academic essay is a different matter from school work, but Adam ended up doing very well.

I asked, during one meeting: "What else can I help you with today?"

"I, er, I'm looking at, er, at top surgery."

I had been researching trans identities as part of my novel. I had an increasing number of friends who identified as trans and/or non-binary, so I knew about top surgery. Adam also wanted masculinising hormones, for which there was a significant waiting list in 2021, let alone now. Trans healthcare had become a political football like no other, with seemingly every side of the political spectrum out to outdo one another when it came to demeaning and devaluing trans healthcare. It was aggravating. But, as a cis man, the most important thing I could have done was to do exactly as I did. I said: "Okay!" and proposed we call an NHS gender identity clinic.

I didn't question Adam's identity or pronouns or the possibility that Adam might be rejected simply for identifying as they/them, for having a boyfriend, or for being autistic (despite the fact that autistic people happen to be over-represented in the trans community, as we are in the queer community at large). I knew all of those things, but I didn't bring them up. We were on hold with different clinics – first for an assessment, then for Testosterone (or T), which would help Adam's mental health.

Uni kept going well. At Adam's university, a huge number of students (and staff!) are queer and neurodivergent. If Adam was going to further socially transition, it was going to be there. By the end of the first year, Adam shared a poem about wanting to be his father's son. "I could always see myself as someone's boyfriend." It was here that I asked: "do you want me to refer to you as a man?"

"Yeah, I think I do."

Both of us were tearing up.

Coming out is not an easy process – trust me, I've been there. It's also one that never stops. When Adam told his family about his plans to change his name again, now to what was clearly a man's name, and the change in pronouns, this wasn't easy. His mother was scared, his father took a very long time to process, and his brother didn't react much at all. He was loved, but change is difficult.

For his second year, Adam moved onto campus. This is where Adam started Testosterone and his full social transition to male. I supported him 100%. He made plenty of friends, too – all of whom were queer and neurodivergent because of course they were. Initially, he'd been terrified. I had a teary phone call with him. His mother was afraid he would change his mind about Testosterone and about not having his eggs harvested before starting hormone therapy. He told me he was overwhelmed and muddled. I'd read about Freddy McConnell and other trans men who'd given birth after transitioning, as well as knowing that plenty of trans men choose to have surgery to remove their ovaries and wombs, since it made them uncomfortable. There was no 'right' way to be a man – just his.

> I asked: "Do you actually want children?"
> "Well. No. No, I don't."
> "Have you discussed this with your boyfriend?"

"He doesn't care, he says that he wants what feels right to me."
"And what feels right to you?"
"I want to go on T now."
"Then that's all that matters."

We discussed it with his mother. She agreed. It was a lot – not just her firstborn going to live away from home for the first time but also starting Testosterone and living as male. Everything was happening all at the same time. Adam needed it, and she knew it. But she was terrified that he was moving too fast. This is common with cis parents of trans children. The reason Adam wanted to start everything at the same time was that he had been thinking about it for years. Parents don't know how long children spend working through their own identities while they're busy raising children who turn out to be a different gender. That is rough and she needed the space to think and recover. What I, as a mentor, could do was what she, as a mother, could not then – be a sounding board in the short to medium term. I agreed with her, giving her time to recover.

One day, Adam asked me: "Jorik, what do you think of spine lengthening?"

"Are you absolutely insane?"

Why change here? Well, because, unlike trans healthcare, spine lengthening is pseudoscientific and dangerous, potentially causing severe problems in later life. Besides, the T would make him grow a little taller, and his mental health would be improving, making him stand up straighter. That was the one thing I said "no" to. Having gone to Steiner school for ten years, I know quackery when I see it. Besides, I soon found out that the height thing was no longer a problem.

"Jorik, guess what? Link from The Legend of Zelda is the same height as me."

End of height dysphoria for Adam.

Months go by. Adam goes to the gym most days. He is on top of his executive function issues. His voice drops precipitously, settling down to an impressive baritone. The Autistic Wellbeing Group starts and Adam is a founding member. He brings his friends along, who all find themselves very welcome in our little Thursday night community. It's special. For a course he's taking, Adam needs to show that he can organise an event. Together, we decide to create an Autistic Pride event. We both take part in its organisation and celebrate Autistic Pride in late April 2023. It was a great success.

After one AutWell (named so by Adam), he asks if he can chat with me one-on-one. Sure.

"I'm going to change my name again."

Okay, what would you like me to call you?

"Well, my current name is a bit too ooh-look-at-me-I'm-trans, so I'm choosing *******."

I hope he appreciates the very non-gender-essentialist man's name I'm using as a pseudonym.

That summer term, he works very hard to get all his assessments done before June, since that's when he'll have top surgery. He got amazing grades.

Surgery itself went well. He spent a few weeks not moving much, since his body needed to recover. Adam's boyfriend was fussing around him when we called, clearly, incredibly proud.

Adam's recovery is swift, and he moves to live with his boyfriend in a city on the coast. He'll do his placement year there, coming back for his final year in 2024. That was tough – another move, a big one. His placement had to change rapidly due to the company he worked for going out of business. But he found a place as an assistant zookeeper, even doing public speaking about his favourites, the wolves. His partner's experience studying acting at a university conservatoire was frustrating. Adam often struggled to know the right things to do and say. He was not hiding that he was autistic, which Adam's boyfriend was. But he was there. They got through it, with time and with love.

We don't often have disagreements, but when we do, we resolve them. I work with other members of his friendship group; we met via AutWell. When there was a serious problem in that group, I could only support people based on what I knew. I tried my best to facilitate and resolve conflicts. No one else could do it, so I did. The problem went away, after many months of bitterness between them. I didn't know about any of the specifics until after everything had ended. Adam was full of rage. I let him have that moment. When we met again, it was fine. He takes time to process things – his life has been full of changes recently, after all. But I am struck by how quickly he returns to his MO: kindness.

Adam and I found our connection fast and easily. After meeting a nervous, anxious person, terrified of the world, there is now a man – gentle, powerful and kind. Do I feel responsible? Not really.

I do feel smug that I've gotten to know someone who can make me laugh so much. That sense of humour was usually hidden. Before one AutWell, we'd decided that we'd all bring something that related to our current special interest. Adam brought a book about *The Legend of Zelda*.

> "What did you bring Jorik?"
> "Honestly, I just forgot. But I think I can just point to everyone here, since autistic people being happy is kind of my special interest."
> "Wait, so your special interest is the friends you made along the way?"

I cried laughing.

Adam is now coming to the end of his degree. Because of his interest in the natural world, he wants to do a postgraduate course in nature writing. He has also started work for student wellbeing, combining mental health awareness raising with the natural world. When he told me that, I was so proud. As for me, I will support him in whichever way I can, if he chooses to keep me around.

3
Marcus

The second student I met was a young man – let's call him Marcus – who was supposed to be studying games design but instead found himself unable to go to classes, eat or sleep because of toothache. It turned out he had two infected molars, one on each side of his jaw. He was in agony. This being Britain in 2021, he wasn't able to book an emergency dental appointment anywhere and wouldn't be able to until three months after we started working together. All he could do was call 111, the not-quite-at-death's-door-yet phone number from the NHS, who told him to "keep trying," which we did, getting put through to an emergency dental clinic seeing NHS patients. However, my student was in the wrong catchment area for emergency dental care. "They should have never forwarded you to us," their receptionist said. She was irritated; apparently they'd tried to do this previously, due to a lack of NHS dental appointments in most of the local area.

The next day he was in agony again. He'd called back to 111, who ended up (again) advising him to buy over-the-counter pain relief, specifically Paramol, a combination of paracetamol and an opiate. For obvious reasons, that was not acceptable.

Marcus' university, initially, believed that by telling him to call 111 when he was in pain, they'd done their job. They had followed the guidebook and taken action by linking him to an organisation that could help him. This is called signposting and is a vital part of student support, I've learned.

Still, my argument was that this was not acceptable. In the UK, duty of care and safeguarding regulations mean that a young person, especially a vulnerable young person, can't be endlessly batted between different organisations and systems with no one ever taking responsibility. The buck must stop somewhere.

I wrote an email to the head of the disability service at this university, stating that not only was this a dereliction of duty but indicative that the systems of support were unable to meet a situation such as this, where NHS healthcare was not able to meet a young person's needs. Everyone knows that dental care in England has become fully inaccessible for all but the rich and fortunate. This student was not. Instead, he was sent from pillar to post and advised to start self-medicating with opiates. Really, not a good look. The buck needed to stop with the university, I wrote in my safeguarding concern.

Later I was phoned by the head of the disability service, who was angry with me. I should not have written this email, nor should I have been advocating for my students. "Yes, I should," I said. "That *is* my job." I started having a minor meltdown in the middle of the street for fear of losing my job only weeks after I started.

Then my line manager, to her unending credit, told this person that I was, in fact, within my rights to advocate for this student and that in this case I was justified in doing so. She later called me up and apologised. That's how the Autistic Wellbeing group was born, which I have been running since December 2022.

Marcus was now at least better supported within the university. His lecturers weren't angry when he was late or looked tired, because there had been some communication from the disability service. He had an emergency dental appointment on the 24th of December, which finally stopped the pain. He later told me that he would 100% have dropped out had I said: "that must be so hard for you", and moved on.

Marcus finally got his teeth sorted in December 2021. Yes, three months after starting university. But still, he's no longer in pain. That's meaningful. Our weekly meetings slowly turn into Marcus expressing his feelings about himself and his course – games design. He wants to be a games designer, but is mindful of the problematic and toxic aspects of the games industry, particularly in its treatment of designers who are themselves minorities. He's autistic and also gay, as well as from a working-class background. Like me, he's the first generation in his family to go to university. Like me, he has a great love and respect for the craft of video games – as with many autistic people, video games present a world we can, even if only briefly, control. Like me, he's found it difficult to accept himself. The meetings we have become one of the only places he lets go, figuring out what exactly he is feeling. Are the meetings therapeutic? Maybe a bit. But my intention was for Marcus to unpack his feelings and understand them as being part of being autistic. He had been diagnosed young and chafed against the notion, even saying: "I'm not sure I've even got autism." He is, however, just as autistic as I am.

Marcus' issue is not just alexithymia, the difficulty of assessing one's own emotional state, but a sense he has to hide who he is and what he's going through. He's making friends – other people on his games design course. Growing up in a large family, Marcus got used to diminishing his own feelings, to not be in other people's way. Our meetings are a place where he can unload. His work starts to become more and more interesting too, though he has complaints about the way the course is run, with few permanent teachers and a focus on group work, pre-planning and documentation that don't fit the thinking style of an autistic designer with aphantasia.

If I tell you not to think of an elephant, what appears in your mind's eye? Exactly. For Marcus, well, nothing does. Marcus is an amazing visual artist, but doesn't think in storyboards and planning. He does not create assets from a predetermined concept; rather, he starts working with rendering software and sculpts out the image, naturally, like Michelangelo looking at a slab of marble, out of which emerges David. This chafes against the expectations of staff, but Marcus does his best to stay on course. For the rest of his first year, he does extremely well, though his life ends up surprising him.

First, a friendship breakup, where Marcus' former friend had a drunken breakdown and verbally attacked his other friends. When I saw Marcus, he was still seething. Then, a surprise. His best friend from his course, who had come out as a trans woman, became more than a friend. They start going out, surprising Marcus most of all. Gender is a soup that I don't understand, nor does Marcus. What matters is that they love each other, in whichever permutation that arises. I was cautiously optimistic when Marcus announced he was moving off campus to live with friends in his second year – I was happy we wouldn't have the fire alarm tearing through my headphones at least once a session anymore. Though I made sure to tell him that I was around if he needed help. Living together with others is rough, even if you know them well.

My anxieties were warranted. By the time second year starts, Marcus, serious about being an adult, applies for part-time jobs. I had my worries and I told him so. His sleeping pattern is not consistent, causing him to experience frequent sleepless nights. Especially when he was in pain during first year, he would regularly not show up for a meeting, and we'd reschedule or start late. I got used to calling Marcus on Discord, because I knew that'd wake him up. He appreciated me doing so. However, now, he was living with house-mates for the first time, doing a full-time course, as well as working 20 hours a week, things were different. I told him problems would arise. He thought he could handle it all. He was wrong.

Marcus first quit his job at McDonald's to join his girlfriend at a warehouse for a major sex toy manufacturer. The atmosphere wasn't silly, but brutally serious. Marcus was let go after a few months, because he was clearly exhausted on the job. Why? He wasn't coping, he wasn't sleeping, and he was taking care of his girlfriend, who was really struggling too. The uni work piled up high, so Marcus and his friends had to force themselves to get the work done before deadlines, pulling all-nighters. Worse, Marcus started leaving my messages unread. He wasn't responding to my meeting requests and frequently wouldn't turn up at all. I hadn't heard from him for a few days when I contacted his university, with whom I continue to have a good working relationship. They started contacting him too, especially since he hadn't been attending classes.

When he turned up he was not in a good way. He had locked himself in his room for days, only coming out to use the toilet and pick up fast food deliveries. He was destroying himself. Why? In order to feel useful and needed, Marcus had been cleaning, cooking and shopping for all the other housemates. No one else was doing so, so he just did it without asking. He's the kind of person who likes a clean room and a clean house. So, he just did it. He was terrified of conflict, too, and because no one was recognising what he was doing, his self-esteem dropped even further.

When Marcus can't keep his own room organised, something is going seriously wrong. He didn't dare turn on the camera at first, but he eventually showed me what his room looked like. He was evidently exhausted, his long hair in a bedraggled ponytail. He was clearly depressed; it came steaming out of his eyes. He hadn't told his girlfriend, who was also not feeling well. She knew that things were bad, but not this bad. Then, in January 2023, one of his housemates told the rest of the house that he was going to leave town. The course had dropped in quality since the first year and he needed a year out to consider his options. That meant everyone needed to find housing for the third year, pronto. Initially, Marcus took responsibility for all his friends upon himself. When I told him he couldn't, he tried to search for housing just for himself and his girlfriend. That added to what was clearly a big depressive episode. Heightened anxiety and a feeling of having failed caused Marcus to feel like he was drowning and retreat inwards, where he stewed, resentful of his own failure as a human being.

Marcus was rarely attending classes now. For several modules, there were no lecturers who could take responsibility for teaching and assessment – that was how severely understaffed the faculty was. Marcus and his friends had all signed up to do a three year course with a one-year professional placement. Of his entire cohort, two found year-long placements, neither of which had anything to do with video game design – one in a school, the other in a shop. This was a huge and evident problem, but not one that the university could technically do anything about. The game industry, Marcus and I knew, was going through a period of transition. More studios were going bankrupt, more people lost their jobs, only for the shareholders to increase their total profits. It became unmanageable for smaller companies to take on students for placements. So, none did.

However, Marcus took all of that as an example of his own failure. He was the one who couldn't get a placement, he was the one who'd been let go from work, he was the one who couldn't control his sleep schedule, let alone his academic performance.

To a non-autistic reader, this emotional state might seem hyperbolic, even unrealistic. But this very blame-centred form of depression is far too common in autistics. We lose joy in the things that used to cause us delight, instead feeling like we have failed those around us. Marcus was in serious danger – if not of doing something bad to himself, then certainly of escalating depression. Suicidal ideation is an act against depression. In a very real way, suicide is a way for an individual to regain control of their existence by dying. But think of depression where suicidal ideation isn't even present – you're just reinforcing your own despair by facing up, again and again, to your own failure as a human being. This is called anhedonia, a Greek term basically describing the opposite of joy. Pleasure is no longer the purpose;

life becomes heavy, one moves through treacle. It is possible to suffer more than death could give you release from. I know. I've been there too. Many, if not most of us have.

First up: Marcus was not going to take responsibility for all his housemates. Second: he was not going to rush to try to get himself and his girlfriend a place. He tried, even viewing a house, but he was refused an opportunity even to say whether he wanted it or not. It ended up being just more insult to injury. In the end, he accepted the university-provided housing, which he, as a disabled student, qualifies for.

However, his sleeping pattern had become even more irregular. His caring responsibilities for his girlfriend and the housing situation took their toll on him. There were moments when he was crying on the phone to his parents. He was no longer able to create games, despite deadlines fast approaching. In the end, he decided to knuckle down and do a 72-hour non-stop crunch to get all the work finished, partly because the lecturers who had to take over the course apparently made last-minute changes to the assessment criteria. He didn't want to do it, especially since he'd previously abhorred crunch culture in the gaming industry. Now he was doing it himself. He struggles with dyslexia, and the writing needed to be done in a format that didn't allow for Marcus' usual spellchecking software. I obviously made my feelings known, but his lecturers did not allow for delayed submissions for group work, so he got to it. He wasn't the only one doing it; his girlfriend and most of his housemates were in the same boat. I don't know about them, but it did him damage. I don't think Marcus ever recovered from this 72-hour period of non-stop working, running on Diet Coke, crisps and sweets in order to just keep going. He passed the second year by the skin of his teeth.

He didn't properly rest during the summer either. He was working full-time in order to make enough money to afford housing in the third year, so he would not have to take on part-time jobs. His sleep was still disturbed. He missed his girlfriend. When he moved in, in September, the passion he once had for his subject hadn't quite dissipated, but his enjoyment of university life had. He was hard up for money, but when his mother sent me his application for a disability benefit, I added my professional opinion that he should indeed receive this. That helped. What didn't help was that throughout the year, Marcus and his girlfriend were up against deadlines they were both too burned out to meet and dealt with all-around lack of support. He would only tell me in dribs and drabs of his anxieties about 'the work', talking about his feelings and unpacking his responses to his overall university experience as we went. There was another period of no news. Then, in the summer of 2024, Marcus called me. It was too much for both him and his girlfriend. They'd never recovered from the periods of crunch. They had spent months going round in circles, without making much progress, trying to eke out a video game without the passion that drove them both to this degree. They had barely left their rooms for months. Marcus hadn't recovered from the depressive episode the year before, and he was actually getting even worse. He needed to go home. We called his mother. He was deeply ashamed, but she was proud of him. I was too. It takes a lot of guts to stand up for yourself and know that you shouldn't put yourself through the torture of trying to create something without having your basic needs met. I made sure he could reach me if he was in crisis. The day on which I helped Marcus and his girlfriend leave university without a degree was the same day on which I went to Esther's graduation.

Marcus and I are still in touch. We speak regularly, every other week or so, to check in on his progress. He took several months off, on the order of his parents, to properly recuperate from his terrible experience at university. He seems to have done so, as has his girlfriend. He needed a lot more support than he received, but there were evident problems with the running of the course itself. That was not his fault, of course, which he's slowly starting to understand now. He's also started, slowly, gently, designing his own games again. When an autistic person loves something really deeply, it's impossible to destroy that love.

I asked Marcus recently about our relationship as mentor and mentee. He said: "When my friends ask me about who you are and what you do, I tell people you're my autistic mentor; like, you've taught me to be autistic. To accept myself. That kind of thing."

When it came to our communication styles, he told me: "When I say: I'm having a yellow kind of day, you'd know exactly what I meant." And I do.

4
Brandon

When I became a tutor, I knew that my relationships with my students were temporary and limited to a single hour a week. Because of who I am, I started slowly losing neurotypical tutees and gaining neurodivergent ones, building relationships that are, in some cases, still ongoing. That was because, somehow, I was able to support neurodivergent students in a way I wasn't able to as easily with neurotypical students. Unmasking, or letting go of the idea that we should be neurotypical, is a vital part of the work I do. It's about making myself vulnerable so the student can, in turn, be truthful. For neurotypicals, this is strange. Why should there be a difference? If you're being professional, you should treat people equally.

Back in 2023, I got into serious trouble after going to a meeting with other mentors at one of the universities my students go to. I told them about the book that you are reading right now. I believe that mentors work best from lived experience – in fact, it's the only reason I am any good at my job. It's precisely because I've experienced higher education as an autistic person that I know how to advise and support others who are currently going through it. This was, it's safe to say, not appreciated. I was the only actually autistic mentor of autistic students present. Others complained about me. Yes, I do feel a bit bitter, but that's what it is. It was a classic case of me not being comfortable in an environment not made for me. The other mentors all believed I was placing myself above them, making out that they were less capable than they were. Well, I was, and I am. To have walked in your mentees' shoes, as it were, makes you a better mentor, especially since the relationships we have are so, so vital.

One student – call him Brandon – had initially thought a neurotypical mentor might be preferable to one with lived experience of being neurodivergent. He essentially wanted to be taught the right (read: neurotypical) way to exist in a university context. It was odd for Brandon to actually be expressing himself honestly and start to understand himself as a disabled person. One day, during those first months as a freshman living on campus, I got a text from him: "Jorik my face has stopped moving." I responded: "What the fuck?!? I'm calling you now." What happened? Bell's palsy, a neurological disorder that often has unknown causes, though it has been found to be a by-product of physical exhaustion. I was happy enough it wasn't a stroke. He went back to his parents' place for a bit.

This situation looked all too familiar. I would get sick a lot more frequently in contexts where I was masking. I remember being in my teens and getting sick with pneumonia, even glandular fever. Why? Burnout. Burnout from people and having to pretend. This student wasn't out as autistic, either to his frat-boy friends or his teammates on the football team. He was studying physics, which was a far less hospitable degree for neurodivergent students than I'd thought. He was living in a very noisy student house, with many apparently necessary parties, late nights and early mornings. He was exhausted, and it was barely November 2021.

We kept on talking. It looked like I'd been right. He told me that he'd been diagnosed relatively young, at five years of age. His parents were advised to get early intervention. Early Intervention is a brand name of ABA, a behavioural modification therapy from which modern conversion therapy arose. Its origins lie in operant conditioning and Pavlov's abusive research on dogs in the early twentieth century. After developing ABA, its Norwegian-American originator Ole Ivar Lovaas joined the so-called 'Feminine Boy Project' in the 1970s, using the behavioural techniques he'd used to make autistic "children indistinguishable from their peers." The Feminine Boy Project took gay boys and trans girls and forced them to behave like heterosexual cisgender males. The few who survived their ordeal said they were still as queer as before Lovaas got his hands on them, just profoundly traumatised. Interestingly, Brandon was the only student I saw in 2021–2022 who was cisgender and straight. Our community sees behavioural modification as torture.

Early Intervention imposes systems of abuse onto very young children, from 18 months onwards, despite its claims of an evidence base. The aim is for autistic children to internalise their sensory and emotional overload, so when they flap their hands, jump or echo in order to self-regulate, they are to be punished. Conversely, when they hide their emotions, speak in a manner that is inauthentic to them and pretend to be 'normal' children, they are rewarded. If this sounds like dog training, you're not wrong. Despite the evidence from the lived experience of the victims of ABA (see Kupferstein, 2018), this is still the only 'support' for autistic people funded by Medicare in the US. Through Autism Speaks and the voices of significant political and cultural figures, ABA *is* what you do to 'combat' autism across the US. Hence the reason many autistics fear coming out as themselves over there – it's simply not safe to be ourselves. The UK mostly uses PBS, another brand name of ABA, with less physical punishment and greater use of shame and social pressure. Very English, you will agree.

Brandon was telling me how he had his hands in his pockets all the time, in order to hide his stims (self-stimulatory behaviours we perform to calm our brains down in states of overload). He had always believed he should be treated in the same way as the other boys in his year and not seek additional support. The Bell's Palsy incident made him think otherwise. It was tough for me too, though I didn't feel emotionally affected until after our call was over. When I was in my early teens, I had several behavioural 'interventions' where I was shamed, humiliated and sometimes hurt in order to "express my emotions in a healthier way". I now have CPTSD. Like me, my student was a victim of conversion therapy. I cannot release him from the self-suppression he was taught at a very early age – though, thankfully, not for very long. It's his fight, though. I can't fight it for him. I can only say that the way these people – professionals! – expected him to behave wasn't acceptable. They will have had the best of intentions towards him; mine certainly did with me. The greatest cruelties come from kindness, after all. He will have to work through his own feelings and allow himself to be more authentic, in his own time. That's a boundary I do impose: I can't *fix* anyone. I can only show what's out there. What matters most is their own capacity to choose the life *they* want.

As I said before, a kind of friendship will develop between mentee and mentor. We both unmask, we both express ourselves honestly, as equals, as adults. That creates a bond. I'm not made of stone. I do refer to my students as 'dude', 'bro', 'man' or 'kiddo' sometimes, because I think it's funny and they told me they do too. Sometimes we have nothing to 'really' talk about, so we share our interests. I talk about books I'm reading, they talk about videos they've watched and music they're listening to. I have my WhatsApp open, even if only for students to complain about how busy the train station is.

Knowing that I can be reached is important. I've never been called in the middle of the night, but I'd prefer it if students call rather than suffer when they're in trouble. I always say: "I'm here", "I work for *you*", and "I don't *want* to post your bail, but I will if I have to". That's obviously meant jokingly, but I do mean it. We as mentors have a very specific but deeply complex job. We are the people the students are going to share problems with first, before teachers, often before their parents, partners and friends. This is a responsibility that I cannot take lightly.

The trick is to focus on the student and *their* wellbeing. It's a kind of friendship but ultimately a one-sided one. I have my own support network. If you want to become a mentor, you need to distinguish the relationships you necessarily build while working in this field from your personal ones. My students are not my friends – they're my employers. I work for *them*.

5
Miles

Miles is a 32-year-old autistic man with lived experience of complex trauma. He's obsessed with politics and wants to make a difference in the world. To us, that's an obvious consequence of living in a world that's unacceptable in its unfairness and cruelty. To people unlike us, that's a 'special interest', a character trait, a frippery, easily dismissed and irrelevant to the wider world. That's until things go bad, and they certainly did go bad in 2023.

We started working together that summer. He wanted to work with an autistic mentor, instead of a neurotypical one, as those had not been good experiences for him. He was focused on a young man in his early twenties he'd been attracted to, deeply, on a emotional level. This man represented something pure, something genuine to Miles – a road not taken, an image of himself without complex trauma. Young, powerful, charismatic, beautiful without the mental scars that came from his childhood.

Miles was previously a shut-in – many of us have periods of excluding ourselves from the world, often for years on end. These people are known in Japanese as *Hikikomori*. Most of them are autistic. I knew Miles processed emotions slowly and blamed himself for not getting social cues. He wanted to connect with the wider activist community at his university but since he was about ten years older than his classmates, they usually met him with a cold shoulder.

In October 2023, I received a video that Miles had shared. He was going to do a hunger strike so his university would describe the genocide in Gaza as such – a genocide. The only problem: no one cared. Unlike hunger strikes happening across the world, there was no support network, no one stepped in to help advocate for him, actually Palestinian activists were confused and perturbed. The activist systems he thought would open up for him once he showed his commitment to the cause stayed shut. What was going on?

He was trying to kill himself in public. I knew it immediately. He had a cause, he was ready to die and, on some level, must have known it was not going to work. There have been many hunger strikes in support of Gazans until the time of writing (late 2024). Some have died for their cause. Nothing has changed, even with the support networks present for those other activists. Calling for a hunger strike as a lone wolf does not make for successful activism. But that wasn't the point.

We had a lot of conversations over the next few weeks. I advised him to take a break, which he did reluctantly and only for a few weeks. In January, he moved to a different city for a placement. The shared housing establishment where he ended up didn't welcome him. They did not appreciate his sense of humour or his activism. They just thought he was weird. For me, that was relatable content. I remember moving house in the middle of a huge emotional breakdown. I, too, pushed people away like a polarised magnet.

After a few months, the placement that, in his eyes, would have allowed him to put his values to work did not live up to expectations. He stopped attending. He cancelled sessions with me. Only when his university started to escalate and threaten to expel him did he call on me. We booked a meeting with his tutor. It hurt, but I knew exactly what Miles had been doing: he was trying to destroy himself again. If he was kicked out of uni, he would not have funding to pay for rent, food and his activism. He was skating close to what, in his eyes, would be classified as complete failure. I remember this need to set fire to everything I'd done, because I didn't get people on my side. I had failed. Not because of what I did, because, fundamentally, I was at fault. I wasn't going to let Miles do the same thing again.

Why didn't he respond to emails? Because he was trying to destroy himself. Why didn't he tell the truth to his counsellor, his placements manager or me? Because he wanted to take sole blame for everything that went wrong. Why did he do all this? Because old hurt, as old and hurtful as it is, is safer than being kind to yourself if all you know is that pain.

He got the opportunity (and funding) to resit the year. I didn't cry until well after the meeting was over. My own therapist pointed out that my own experience, being autistic and having complex PTSD, gave me a deep well of wisdom and empathy to help prevent others from destroying themselves in the same ways that I tried to. Of course, I baulked (barfed!) at the idea that I had any wisdom whatsoever. But, unfortunately for my ego, my therapist was right. Having the specific lived experience of complex trauma and being autistic, I *do* recognise the behavioural consequences of that pain. I don't just recognise it, I feel it, deeply. That's the power lived experience brings. It has a cost, but, my God does it have a benefit.

6
Lissa

I was Lissa's third mentor in as many years. She had seen one for a few weeks in her first year and then another only once in her second. Both mentors were female, cis, likely heterosexual, and neurotypical. She stopped seeing both after a few sessions. Lissa told me in our first meeting about her experiences with both of them. "Oh, you made a joke! I… didn't know you people could do that!" and "Who did you get to paint your nails?" "I did it myself." "You're lying." These two well-meaning white women, probably straight, definitely cisgender, were too concerned with what they believed to be true about autistic people to see reality. No, we *can* paint our own nails, and we *can* make jokes. It's how Lissa and I communicated. She's hilarious.

Mainstream culture, especially mainstream views of what autistic people are *supposed* to be, has a way of describing us back to ourselves, relying entirely on hurtful, stereotypical descriptions. As autistic people, we have to constantly argue with the stereotypes – stereotypes, usually created and reinforced by specific people for specific purposes. That's no accident. There is a real value to prejudicial views on what autistic people are (and aren't) supposed to be. Yes, there's the empathy thing, as ever. It seems vital for a non-autistic society to conceive of certain other people as an empty box, devoid of what makes *themselves* human. This is due, again, to the double empathy problem. Since our intuitive, emotional empathy is often painfully huge, we struggle, however, with intuitively empathising with non-autistics. We are, as indicated by research from Sasson (2017) and others, highly empathetic. The empathy gap lies not with us, though, but with the majority neurotype. This is neurochauvinism, upheld by those very stereotypes. As I discuss in *Feeling Fast and Slow*, the system of anti-autistic discrimination has very little to do with our actual experience of the world, and far more with the *perception* of the majority neurotype, based in their own sense of superiority. Basically: the majoritarian neurotype requires an underclass: if good people are good *because* they are empathetic, then autistic people are evil because they are devoid of empathy, pathologically self-interested: hence the name 'autism' - the disorder or diseased state of the - *autos* - or self'. Obviously, their confident use of these stereotypes made Lissa immediately suspicious of her previous mentors.

Lissa was at the end of her degree in Classics, in her third year, at a large university. When we started, she had just begun a leading position at her drama society. It was scary, especially since she was being watched from all sides. Still, this was her space. She was in charge. She was autistic, and as a former drama school student, I was 95% incredibly proud of her and 5% a little disturbed by how confident she was as a director. I couldn't have imagined being as in control and self-assured as she was, having been to drama school myself in the mid-2000s, in the Netherlands. Truly, things have changed for autistic people who make theatre since I was a drama student, aeons ago, to see that an autistic person could do well in theatre, rather than be excluded for neurochauvinist reasons. As for me, I was defeated back in 2006, so my first impression was: '*Oh, she's just better than I was when I was 20. Maybe I was just incompetent, rather than the victim of ableist treatment.*' But even then, that was only 5%.

In the first week of term, that self-assurance was challenged. During an event for new students, a male student – one of the people running auditions for another drama society that day – was accused of inappropriate behaviour towards female auditionees. One of these was part of Lissa's society. She was enraged. She felt powerless to stop it from happening in the first place. This happened in a shared space, a place she'd always seen as safe, secure from abuse like this. Harvey Weinstein wannabes have no place in the environment where she and her friends made art. She said: "I don't know what I need to do about this. People are asking me for solutions."

I proposed one: "Let this anger fuel you. Make something out of this, that's both an opportunity for learning and a space to work through your righteous anger." She did.

In January, her show about male radicalisation and online antifeminism played at her student union. My partner and I went to watch. It was really special. It was a huge production. The plot could have been more intense and focused, which she agreed with. But the show was a devised piece, co-created by the cast, this included dramaturgy. Therefore, the plot of the show and its characters were created by the cast.

Despite that, her preparation process had been state-of-the-art. In November 2021, she booked a meeting with me where she would interview me about toxic masculinity and incels. I had been doing a lot of reading about reactionary politics and the place of neurodivergent people in those movements (usually, as cannon fodder). When it came to autistic boys, I know from experience, having taught boys who had been radicalised by online communities. What all of them had in common, was a struggle to understand why they, as white, (supposedly) cishet autistic teenage boys were excluded from racial patriarchy while they were white and male. Simply arguing that their behaviour was misogynist wouldn't make them budge. What did, however, was a greater understanding of how society already works. They can then accept that they are disabled and (very likely, looking at the numbers!) queer in some way, connecting with others against a system that is unfair to minorities. Or, what happens more often – at least initially – is that they are caught up in an ideological system that is decentralised (often taking place on anonymous forums), keeps the current system intact (*why do these other nerds get to be so successful?*) and answers their questions directly. '*Why can't I get a girlfriend?*' '*Because your face is the wrong shape*' (see Wynn, 2018 and Srinivasan, 2022). Their own lack of attractiveness is not due to any overriding systems in society, but due to something inherent and unique to them. The last 15 years have seen an increase in Incel (involuntary celibate) violence across the world, and their connections to different parts of the far right can no longer be ignored. We will return to incels and online radicalisation later on.

Lissa is a gay woman herself and has strong views on cishet patriarchy and the dangers of male violence. Her anger will lead – and has led – to beautiful art. I didn't pull away from the painful reality of her position somehow being damaged, even if that would mean engaging with a painful part of her life – and mine, for that matter! I didn't want to distract her from the very real issues that have come on her path. So, I advised her to step up to the plate.

She did. Amazingly. The final question in her survey was: "How do we deradicalise young men?"

The big one. I responded with: "Erm… Gay sex?"

She laughed, but I wasn't joking. When it comes to autistic people, the vast majority of us are queer. If we engage with other autistic people, we will definitely have queer friends. Heteronormativity does not fit us, or who we are. It didn't for me, nor any of my male autistic friends. We were more right-wing when we were younger, believing the far-right's propaganda about our inherent failure of masculinity. We were bitter. I was bitter. Many autistic boys were in the same situation in their teenage years. I was a teenager before the online far right blew up like it did in the 2010s. I never interacted with any forums; I was just busy hating myself 24/7, 365. One of my friends was an Incel, actually, until she came out as trans. Now she's an out, proud lesbian, leftist and queer rights activist. Another read the manifesto of Elliot Rodger when he was in his late teens and came to the conclusion: "Oh jeez – he's trying to brainwash me!" He still didn't have a girlfriend and wouldn't for a while, but he did end up coming out as bisexual. A surprise for him, but not for his family, or friends. For me, when I stopped forcing myself to be straight and instead "let go" (I experienced it as a "giving up" on passing as "normal". I was a messy boy), I lost my reactionary streak soon after.

> "By that I mean: autistic incels are likely queer anyway. That will allow them to deradicalise, as they suddenly discover that they do have a community. For neurotypical incels, I have no idea. I worry about them. And us."

She used this survey to scaffold her process. The show did amazing work and was a wonderful piece of political theatre: funny, exciting, excellently staged and multi-faceted. She made it work for her. On the night, I told her how proud I was and asked if I could give some feedback on the dramaturgy. She said: "I am not capable of receiving any feedback from other people right now, but thank you." This was completely understandable: she was dealing with so much more input, praise, other people's feedback, lights, needing to give notes to the cast, etc. ad infinitum. We discussed it in a later meeting, no problem.

About a month after that, she messaged me, saying that her uni was going to kick her out. Why? She had been really struggling attending lectures. Since 2021, the habit of recording lectures and allowing students to stream them was slowly phased out at Lissa's uni, even though certain students' disability support plans mandate this as an accessibility requirement. Lissa is very sound-sensitive, especially when she's tired. She couldn't handle the creaky noise of old seating and endless conversations around her that wouldn't allow her to concentrate on what the lecturer was actually saying. There was also executive functioning: the magnitude of her other responsibilities meant that there were days when the number of people she had to work with and consider just exhausted her. Lissa was relying on these recordings. If she'd had a rough day at drama society the night before, she would tune in via video. When that stopped happening, she still did the reading, of course, but didn't manage to go into lectures. Instead of responding to our emails, the university unilaterally started holding students accountable for their (lack of) attendance.

The email came through. She needed to meet with a member of staff, since she was facing expulsion. I was pissed. So was Lissa. I couldn't make the meeting with her uni staff, but she ably defended herself, simply pointing at her disability access document, which had *never* been fully integrated into the teaching she received. Despite her diagnoses not having changed, she needed to send medical evidence for every extension request she ever submitted. Lissa started her degree in 2019, moving back home for obvious reasons in early 2020. Her third year was the only one that she lived away from her parents full-time.

Many students were put in precarious positions due to Covid; there was a movement against universities only providing online, not face-to-face tuition during the pandemic. Therefore, some said, universities shouldn't charge the same amounts as they would for regular, in-person teaching. There's a good argument for that. Going to university is far too expensive anyway, and lockdown learning was a depressing ersatz way of studying without the chance to fail at being an adult that in-person university would provide. However, the tuition fees students pay (nearly always in loans) don't even begin to cover the costs of that single student studying for a year – the rest is made up by the education ministry.

For the people complaining about online-only tuition, it must have been good that in-person teaching became the norm again at Lissa's university. However, when making those decisions, no one was concerned with disabled students and staff. Sometimes, our bodies and brains do not allow us to come to work or university. That's okay – it's called *'being disabled'*. However, when we hold students responsible for attending – let alone attending in the 'right' way – we are imposing our own ideas onto them. We're autistic. Sometimes we're just overloaded and need to stay inside and play *Animal Crossing*. When we feel a bit better, we can access the lectures when we are able. This is why autism often can functionally resemble a chronic illness.

I get the university lecturers' point of view: what if the university just reuses lectures from previous years, so it can fire lecturers as a cost-cutting exercise, slowly turning university education into Netflix with a £9,250 annual subscription fee? I completely agree, that *is* what most universities are working towards, as part of the structuring of education to be more and more like paid content consumption. It's my responsibility as someone working at universities to be aware of current pressing issues, to understand wider political and systemic problems in the sector, so as to best support my students. I don't just want to tell students that their lecturers are wrong, nor do I want to tell the students that they should just, y'know, attend more lectures. Especially if they struggle with that due to their stated and registered disability.

Instead, Lissa was nearly expelled. The reason she wasn't, was due to the university's final term being nearly at an end and her results. For the course she faced expulsion for, she got a first class honours result (an A or A*). For another course, featuring intense collaboration with other students, she got through by essentially doing all the work herself. That used to be my MO for group work too. I can't stand group work; it's the social interaction and accountability part that costs me far more effort and energy than simply doing it myself. Despite her working herself to the breaking point, she got an amazing result for her degree.

She did not want to be a classicist, though. Lissa is a theatre maker, desperate to go into theatre professionally. She was nervous, but, with my encouragement, she applied for an MA in theatre directing at a large drama school in London. She picked my brain while she was working on her cover letter. I said: "be honest. Use the show about male violence against women as an example." A few weeks later, I got the text.

"I got in!!!"

I met Lissa again in August; her show was playing for a week at the Edinburgh Fringe Festival. Now, I went to the Edinburgh Festival every year from 2009–2013. I knew how the Fringe had evolved and what it used to be. I can recall the youth hostels on Cowgate, the smell of hops in the air, the noise at night. I was there, trying to be a stand-up comedian, but never getting anywhere. In 2009, I recall, her university was represented by no fewer than 6 shows, all with casts, directors, producers, techs and flyerers, for the full stretch of the festival. There were improv and sketch groups, as well as students doing runs at the Free Fringe and Free Festival off their own backs. Not anymore. 2022's Fringe was the first real return for the festival since 2019. Both 2020 and 2021 were cancelled or radically decreased in size. The cost of running a show was far higher now. Rents, already out of control in 2009, were even more extortionate. I travelled to Edinburgh from London on an overnight coach for £18 return in 2009. Now you won't get out of London for that money. Lissa's show only ran for two weeks. The actors were also tech and crew, as well as flyering. The Royal Mile was surprisingly quiet. I was in Edinburgh giving a talk on autism and neurodiversity, taking the staff of the business I spoke for to Lissa's show. The room was (nearly) full, but not filled to the rafters as it had been when I saw plays there in 2009 and 2010. The show was beautifully written, magical. I was so proud of her. I told her that over coffee in a café on the Royal Mile.

Lissa was, in her own words, "fucking exhausted." She needed to move to London, but she knew that she'd manage there. "These are my people." Her term started just after her Fringe run ended. She said she wouldn't need mentoring, so she wouldn't apply for disability support allowance or reasonable adjustments. The application process was "just one more thing I can't handle right now." Besides, I couldn't do it for her. I wasn't going to. I was happy to finish our work there.

I didn't hear from Lissa for a few months, until December 2022. Things were not going well. We had a number of meetings to help her find support with the ongoing issues she was facing in drama school. We got in touch with the UK Student Loans Company, who are responsible for Disability Support Allowance, so she would get funding for travel in London – which I would have benefited from myself had I known of its existence. I hated travelling in London when I was a student there. We tried to find people to mediate on the conflict she had with a classmate, an autistic man who was treating her in a way that was not acceptable. The school wasn't able to provide the support she needed. In fact, even after I gave a talk to its staff, there was little or no improvement for Lissa and when she asked, I helped her write a letter to the school to request an interruption of studies.

She was not doing well. She had tried to engage with drama school as a place where her people were. When it wasn't, that was rough. 'I don't want to have to be a trailblazer, I just want to be a theatre director.' Hopefully, having taken out some time to rest, she'd eventually be able to return to London and find the environment she deserves.

Lissa and I didn't speak for over a year. She needed time away. I, of course, felt a bit triggered by that rejection. Had I been living out my own failed ambitions in Lissa? Maybe, but I don't think I was. I just knew that she wanted to be a theatre director with all her heart and I supported her to the best of my abilities. I didn't lie to her, I didn't say that her time there was going to be easy. But when she told me that the industry had moved on in the way disabled people were represented, I decided to believe her. It was all I could do. Maybe she was disappointed in me, that I didn't manage to keep her safe. I did my best, but sometimes, the system still wins. I can't – and I shouldn't – try to protect students from that. They are adults and make their own choices. All I can do as a mentor is support what the student wants to do. I don't provide uncritical support, but I also don't impede on the student's own capacity to make choices for themselves. Whether she is or isn't disappointed in me, I'm definitely not disappointed in her. She's amazing, she's so young still, she's only in the early stages of her career, and I wish her all the best. And sometimes, that's how it should end.

Lissa Post-Script:

> Despite my anxieties, I found out that she absolutely had not been disappointed in me at all. I contacted Lissa after writing this chapter, which she gave feedback on. She is still dealing with the effects of long-term burn-out, but also managed to graduate drama school. She told me that, despite her initially saying that she didn't want to be a trailblazer, just a theatre director, that was not what she meant. She says: "I think I did say this, but reflecting on it what I really meant was: I don't want to be *forced* to be a trailblazer. I want that to be my choice."

She's right. Her response is so empowering. In order to make art that is authentic, genuine, political and beautiful, we have to feel we can build freely. The knowledge that we can choose our own battles is a vital one for disabled or otherwise minoritised artists. We cannot constantly work with the neurotypical gaze in mind. If we are going to make art we are proud of, we have to be able to start from a place of strength, a foundation, to later build something on. When we have to state and restate that we are human, as yet another price to pay in order to make art, that is just one more thing we have to deal with, instead of making something that we actually want to make. We should be allowed to succeed and fail on our own merits, not those of a drama school or university. As artists, we deserve that space, community and validation. We should be allowed to be as boundary-breaking as we want, not simply by virtue of who we are. Instead, who we are should nourish and stabilise the art we hope to make. Likewise, I am confident Lissa will find herself in rehearsals again soon, blazing trails and breaking boundaries. I'll be watching with interest.

7
Esther

The first time I met Esther was over Zoom. That was how we would be meeting for her entire degree. She was 18, studying sociology, had just left the Home Counties to study in the West of England. She moved onto campus and tried to get herself in order. I knew I had enough background in sociology, having studied journalism for a while and being a committed socialist. I'd done my reading. When I asked Esther what she wanted to do after her degree, she didn't know. But in October 2021, I was struggling enormously and had to take a week off for my mental health, which, *touch wood*, hasn't been as bad since. When I got back to work, Esther told me that things weren't great. What was going on?

She told me that she was going to lectures, as overwhelming as those were. She was trying to retain as much information as possible. Where she was not doing well was in reading. As in: she had not read a syllable. Why not? Esther is dyslexic. She hadn't communicated this to the disability service. At all. We contacted the disability service together, things were put in place. I started reading her emails with her, which remained unopened in her inbox since September. Whenever we'd meet, we'd start by saying: "Emails?" "Emails!" and we'd read the emails, sort through which ones were important and which ones irrelevant. It sounds patronising to simply read emails with a student, but I've been so anxious that I couldn't read my own emails. Having someone with me to read emails together would have done me a lot of good when I was a student.

Esther's talent, beyond what most sociology undergrads come into their degrees with, is an amazing faculty with numbers and large amounts of data. This is a USP that I've tried to nurture as much as I can. What I can do, however, is limited by my own dyscalculia. I don't do numbers, like Esther can. But even then, I could highlight her talent in that field. On days where she wasn't feeling too confident, she might message me and I'd message back. There were gaps when we weren't speaking much, particularly during the summer, but Esther always knew I was there.

Second year was intense. She moved to live with her friends in the centre of town. Esther got her first ever job, with my help. She had never written a cover letter or a job application. Job applications are the worst. They demand a really weird middle-ground in the way that you have to be confident in your tone but not conceited. Even when the job was a cleaning job in a pub, so early mornings. You need to be clear about your capacities but also bigging yourself up just enough that you're neither too keen nor a total bullshitter. Worst of all, most of the time, neither application form nor cover letter are actually read by the staff that's hiring you. Which partly leads to why, in the UK, only 3/10 autistic people are employed. That's insulting. We have a lot of work to do, and the increased amount of admin we need to do in order to be allowed to even *start* is not helping.

At the start of second year, Esther told me she had started to date someone, a girl she'd met around the start of the year. I was so proud of her, and told her so. This was her first serious relationship, too.

For one of her modules she had no idea how to go about the very specific piece of writing she was expected to do. I would have helped, but despite asking them if I could, her university did not allow me to work with Esther as a Study Skills tutor as well as a mentor. Why? Because my provider hadn't cleared me for doing so. Instead, because Esther didn't want another mentor, be that someone allocated by her uni or another – very probably neurotypical – study skills tutor, she had no study skills support. Knowing the level of people who worked with my other mentees, I get why she chose not to.

When she got her grade back, it was the first time she'd failed a course. We got in touch with staff, surely there were problems with accessibility across the module. The answer: no, not really. Not this time, at least. The course leader was also dyslexic, the course tutor was autistic. It was a bit awkward, and I felt embarrassed about highlighting ableism. I was wrong to feel that way, though. The issue remains that Esther was prevented from accessing the module equally, because of circumstances outside of the control of the teaching staff. Esther chose not to work with uni-provided writing support, nor with a study skills tutor who wasn't me. To the university, they had provided her with more than enough accessibility options. It just didn't work.

Here's another example of where breaking the rules would have been beneficial. We know that universities have rules. We also know that those are beneficial to neurotypical students and staff, since they are the majority neurotype. Therefore, when it comes to adjustments, what the student needs, not what is already available, should be of primary importance. If Esther wanted to work with someone she already knew, that should have been the most important consideration. I get why universities have rules and standards in place to protect their students. But here, breaking the rules to the advantage of the student would have been, clearly, more ethical than not having done so.

Luckily, she only failed that single module. Esther's university's rules allowed for a single module to be failed out of all taken during a degree. Wait, am I saying that when a rule benefits disabled students, it's fine, but when it doesn't, it's bad? Yes. Yes I am. That's not hypocritical. My intention is that the students get the results that they deserve, knowing that they are likely to have lower grades because of how unequal the world is. But I would go further. If by a horrible bit of luck, I *somehow* get to be in charge of universities, I would do away with all exams, and yes, that includes essays. They stand in the way of genuine learning. I have never learned more than when I was learning out of interest and fascination. This may be an autistic thing, but I learned far more in my own time, just from reading for pleasure. I would have finished secondary school far earlier, with far less exhaustion, burnout and heartache, if I had been allowed to do my own thing, learning from home. Being in a school, around other human beings, prevented me from learning. If that sounds strange to you, I'm definitely not the only autistic person who sees school that way.

In short: yes, tests, exams, essays and projects – particularly group projects – are actively detrimental to autistic people's natural learning strategies. In an acceptable world, we would be able to acquire knowledge for its own sake, at our own speed, in our own way. *We* are already making adjustments *for neurotypicals*, simply by the way university courses operate.

But how can we know that someone's degree is worth anything without a grading system? Well, one of my best friends (autistic, obviously) has a first-class PhD in mathematics from Oxford University and has been unemployed for a year, after four years of fully-paid post-doctoral positions. Why? Because of the issues I highlighted earlier with job applications. It's a system that seems invented for the purpose of excluding autistic people from the workplace. It doesn't matter how capable we are, we don't get the jobs that we actually deserve. Meritocracy is dead, if it was ever real in the first place. So we might as well learn for the sake of it. League tables be damned.

Back to Esther. I woke up with a text from her, early in the morning. She had been to a party in a club the night before, where she had been spiked. Her drink? No, someone put a needle in her arm and injected drugs into her, while she was in a busy area. I know, I swore too. She was at A&E overnight and was allowed to go home in the early hours of the morning. Her mates were going to be there to support her.

Not too long after that, it was the Christmas break. I hadn't heard from Esther for a while. What happened? She had a breakup. Now, your first proper breakup is rough, but this one was particularly hard. She felt humiliated. And she was right to feel that way.

At our first meeting, it was rough. I hadn't seen her in that bleak a state since she told me she had forgotten to notify the uni about her dyslexia, back in first year. This, though, was more difficult to solve. You can't fix a broken heart with text-to-speech software, no matter how hard AI evangelists are going to try.

However, the way she expressed her grief was not typical. She struggled to verbalise what it was she felt. There was a flatness, that she couldn't put words to. It stuck around, too. For months. After a few months of me gently proposing that she talk to someone, she ended up doing so. "But what do I say?" she asked. I told her about alexithymia. I experience it too. Alexithymia is common in autistic people and people with complex PTSD (I'm both, because I'm just that special). It's when we struggle to ascertain what it is we're feeling, put to words what those feelings are and how they affect us. It goes a lot further than "I'm sad", it's figuring out that 'sad' is how you're feeling in the first place. Our feelings are built up of different layers: physical sensations, intuition, thinking patterns, moods, deeply undergirded by intergenerational pain and complicated feelings that may belong to us, or to other people. I talk more about alexithymia in *Feeling Fast and Slow*.

As for Esther, she wasn't able to verbalise what felt to me painfully obvious. Her friends agreed. She wasn't in a good way. After a few months, she did decide to see a counsellor, provided not by her university or the NHS, but by the municipality of her university town. This was a great decision from her. I helped by clearly laying out how to address alexithymia with her counsellors. Mainstream counsellors, like the ones provided by NHS services or universities, are mostly taught to think in behaviour-first models. If you are sad, that is because you're not doing enough things to make you not-sad. Change the behaviour and: hey presto! Mental wellbeing achieved. Obviously, it's not so simple, despite the entirety of mainstream mental health treatment being aligned to this system in one way or another. Great that it's also amazingly detrimental to autistic people, but that seems to be a feature, not a bug.

By the way, to Lissa's previous mentor: that was a joke. We can do those.

Esther started her third year more confidently and, I found out, was now together with her girlfriend. She was the same age but had taken two years out, so she was in first year. Esther was leaving town at the end of the year. What would she do? I proposed several times to start looking at postgraduate courses or jobs that would have allowed her to stay in town. But anxiety took over. She couldn't do it. Not right now. I said: "Okay, but please focus on what you can do right now. Focus on your dissertation." She did. She ended up getting a 2:1, the second-highest grade for a UK university degree. My god, I was proud of her. She'd told me her parents wanted to meet me at her graduation. I travelled up, she looked stunning, even if her graduation cap kept falling off. I spoke to her parents, making them laugh. Her dad looked at me, beaming with pride and gratitude. But I told him: this is not me. She did this. All I did was tell her that she was right. She deserved to succeed. Now, she had. He said, Esther looking at him: "Esther's mother and I were thinking, would it be possible for Esther to train as, well, as a Jorik?" But how would she train for that? Well friends, you're currently reading that book.

I still see Esther regularly as she's applying for graduate jobs, funded through Transition Mentoring. Together, we attack the shitness of job applications, interviews and life admin. Those things are best done together, not apart. I look forward to seeing Esther, someday, if she wants to, become a Jorik in her own right. Or, even better, be someone else's Esther.

8
Daisy

Sometimes, a student comes along who breaks all the rules right back at you. All you can do is figure things out to the best of your capacities, but, in lieu of better options, also know when to step away.

Daisy was in her second year, studying biology. When we started, she was undiagnosed as autistic. She never thought she could be, her university had proposed she get autism mentoring because it was clear she was struggling. Not with her course – no, she was always getting outstanding grades. She was highly motivated and can hyperfixate on something, explaining to me just how cool a particular micro-organism is. She is also one of the funniest people I'd ever met. However, aside from her parents and her brother when she travelled home from uni, she had no social contacts. None. She had no friends, no group of people she would hang out with at uni, didn't have a job. She despised her first-year housemates and hated the lady she was a lodger with, all of whom, to my knowledge, were only obnoxious in just how neurotypical they were. And yes, to give Daisy credit, they were deeply neurotypical.

The way in with her was through humour. We made each other laugh. She has an incredibly dark sense of humour, self-effacing and with a potty mouth unexpected from a short, curly-haired girl with glasses. She genuinely outswears me. And I can swear!

But where Daisy made me work was by just how pliant she was. She didn't *want* to discuss much of anything. Nothing much ever went on in her life, according to her own telling. The anecdotes she did tell me seemed hyperfocused on trying to make me laugh – which she always succeeded at. But I'm nothing if not a good listener. I would always be able to pick out from the wall of snark whatever showed what she was really going through. Lecturers were difficult. They seemed to have a real gift for devaluing what she did. Group projects were hell – she would just do all the work and let others take the credit. Her housing situation was atrocious. She did not feel at home in her lodgings. Her landlady had the terrible habit of treating her like a long-lost child, which gave Daisy the ick.

Daisy would go home every weekend, to the rural village where she grew up, near a town well-known for being 'rough'. In the UK, when we're referring to somewhere rough, there's a clear classism at work, yes, but if you're 5 foot and a woman, you're not safe from drunk guys going after you. So her mother would pick her up.

Daisy's family is working class, which is great. My family is working class too. But hers is more riven with the negative social stereotypes of working class people, particularly in this country. Her dad is a small business owner, with a temper and traditional (read: reactionary) views of women's roles. Her mother worked in a shop, at minimum wage, because she was unsure of her visa and immigration status. She would also frequently get angry with Daisy, for a variety of things, primarily her *"not being normal"*, which included Daisy's fawning demeanour towards everyone around her.

What Daisy did, apart from study obsessively, was to write. She wrote a tonne of fan fiction and uploaded it on *Archive of Our Own*, but I've never been able to find any of her work. According to Daisy, that's because she deleted it. I tried to encourage her to share her work, but she never read anything to me. Reason? "Cringe." Fair enough, but she was underselling herself. Whenever I would talk about my own writing, she'd be massively supportive. If I had a bad day or was under the weather, she was deeply empathetic towards me. Yes, she had a sharp tongue, but never at me. I would always try to find something I could do to help her with. But no, she would always say no. There was never a problem with anything, I shouldn't worry. 'It's *fiiiiiinnnneeee*' became the bane of my life for a while. Writing, for her, was something embarrassing that she did, more out of habit than art, without intending to show it to anyone. What I did manage to find out was that she wrote romance. Not uncommon for aromantic and asexual people – Alice Oseman, of Heartstopper fame, found success doing the very same thing. Why not Daisy?

Why would someone so clearly talented, funny, capable and committed be so dismissive of their own needs? Trauma manifests itself in a variety of highly individual ways, so it's difficult to be specific and generalised at the same time. But, on the whole, four different styles of immediate responses to threat can be distinguished. You will have heard of 'fight' and 'flight'. When we're faced with a threat, the basal elements of our brain have to make decisions, and make them fast. Ascertaining whether a threat can be overcome or we need to run away is a choice we make intuitively. The creatures whose intuitions weren't as effective would soon disappear from evolutionary history. Another so-called trauma response is 'freeze'. We know what this looks like in nature: a rabbit or a deer in the headlights, a fainting goat, camouflage for insects, birds and reptiles. Freezing is a highly effective way of avoiding threats without expending the energy that fighting and fleeing would entail.

The fourth, lesser-known trauma response is 'fawn'. Of course a fawn is a baby deer. But the verb 'to fawn' describes behaviour that is actively submissive, even manipulatively so. It's a cat being a little baby by meowing – wild cats don't meow beyond their first few weeks of life, so adult pet cats who meow are infantilising themselves for a clear purpose: '*help me*'. It's a dog rolling on its back. It's also a human being dismissing their own bodily and emotional needs, just to not be in the way, just to not be a problem, just to not be harmed by others.

I have CPTSD. The fawn response is one that I used to show in order to make other people feel comfortable around me so I could run away without losing face socially. I don't know if you recall, but being a child is absolutely terrifying. Add to that being a Dutch child who's clearly gay and obviously autistic in the 1990s. My environments were not safe. I was regularly homophobically abused, by strangers and schoolchildren alike. I didn't even know what a homosexual was, until I was repeatedly told I was one. In order to survive, I started to hide myself behind a series of masks, just to remain safe. I taught myself to read when I was 3. I was bullied as a consequence – yes, that early. I pretended I didn't care about the things I actually cared about, in order not to be at risk. Denying my own needs and the things that gave me joy in life were to be avoided if I didn't want to be hurt.

Daisy was something else, though. When we had a meeting, it was like I got an hour-long private comedy special. I sometimes felt like she was the professional and I the service user. I was honest with Daisy. She said: "Okay, maybe there's something you can do." Daisy has Raynaud's syndrome, which causes severe pain in people's extremities due to a lack of circulation and, in the end, necrosis. Yes, bits of her fingers and toes were going white, then yellow, then blackish. It's not pretty and requires taking good care of yourself, which the anaemia didn't help with. Add to that, she was in recovery from eating disorders and couldn't cook food in her landlady's kitchen because she couldn't stand being around her. She barely ate, controlling food was a way she could control herself even if she couldn't control anything else.

I offered to help her get a doctor's appointment for the Raynaud's, which she wasn't diagnosed with, as well as a blood test and also help with accommodation. She couldn't make herself food in her landlady's kitchen, lived off fruit and a small meal once a day she would defrost when her landlady wasn't in and she was too anxious to buy food when she was at uni. When I went to meet her on campus, we met in one of the cafés. That was genuinely the first time she'd ever been inside the Student Union. "Would you like something? It's on me," I offered. "No, thanks. Thanks for the offer, though!" The doctor's appointment did not end up happening after all. Slowly, through many many meetings, it became clear how much anxiety was controlling her life. She would sometimes send me a message, talking about things being unbearable, then delete them before I had a chance to see them. The first year, she ended up pushing herself through it, mostly not taking my advice on doctors, psychological support (such as anti-anxiety medication, which does me the power of good), her eating or engaging with people outside of her family and, well, me.

The one thing she did engage with was the university's request she seek an autism diagnosis. I never doubted that she was autistic, as much as she still did. Why? Because autism describes being a certain kind of person, rather than a particular set of diagnostic check boxes. I talk about this a lot more in *Feeling Fast and Slow*, but, in brief, the phrase 'I am autistic' is an identity statement. It tells others what kind of person you are and what community you belong to. This is a community without clear boundaries based on the way people look, behave or exist in the world. We are born autistic, our brains definitely diverge meaningfully from the vast majority of human brains – though exactly how we may never find out. In the meantime, Damian Milton's concept of the Double Empathy Problem helps. Despite cultural and diagnostic expectations, autistic people are hugely empathetic. Painfully so, at times. From Greta Thunberg at the UN to Chris Packham on BBC's Springwatch to a multitude of actually autistic artists, musicians and historical figures who are, fundamentally, distinct to the norm of what human beings are supposed to be. We feel very deeply (usually not for ourselves, but for others). To live autistic is to be a part of a complex web of feelings, often to the exclusion of our own. Yet we are defined by centuries of cultural products and a psychopharmaceutical industry as harmful, dangerous and potentially contagious. At the time of writing, Robert F. Kennedy Jr is Trump's nominee for US Federal health minister. Kennedy is a known conspiracy theorist who defended Andrew Wakefield's MMR vaccine hoax.

Wakefield is a disbarred former gastroenterologist from the UK who fraudulently published on the measles, mumps and rubella vaccine purportedly 'causing' autism, so he could sell his own measles vaccine instead. Wakefield was a guest at Trump Tower at his 2016 election win. Now, Kennedy is bringing the autism vaccine myth to the core of American health policy. We clearly have a lot of fighting left to do.

As for Daisy, who is half-American, empathy has never been a problem for her. She is invariably kind and empathetic. Towards me, never herself. This hurt. I was an anxious, high-performing child who was terrified of upsetting anyone. I now know that there was more going on than just an anxious or avoidant personality, or the 'shy'-label, most of which hide far deeper problems. I was deemed 'too good for this world' by friends' parents, even if those 'friends' often couldn't stand me without quite knowing why. I never could either. I was probably just the problem. And then the cycle starts back up again. I did the exact same thing, for years, that I now saw her do. I also knew immediately that we were the same kind of person.

What our meetings became was, frequently, a bit disturbing to me. I would ask her about her week, she would be hilarious, then something would come out that I would pick up on, I would ask whether she wanted me to action something, write an email, book a meeting or call so we could get something off the ground – y'know, like I did with everyone else? The answer was always "no, thanks. I'm fine!" She knew she wasn't. But that wasn't the point. She genuinely believed she couldn't get better. Nothing would ever improve. Either she'd get married to a drunk who'd beat her and be murdered by him, or she'd go and live in her parents' house until they passed and then die at the age of 48, alone and unmissed. No one would care, nothing could be done. Not by me, not by anyone. Suicidal thoughts, but then something truly hilarious afterwards.

It hurt. I was like that once, not even that long ago.

Was she lying? No, I don't think so. She genuinely felt this way. She felt it was genuinely impossible that she would be treated with a smidge of the kindness with which she treated me.

Of course, I tried to reach out, but the company I worked for at first was not safe. I did not feel secure that Daisy would be understood by any staff member there. I sometimes tried to raise concerns subtly, without her finding out, but there was only so much I could do without the student initiating anything, or being aware of something happening for their benefit.

What was even more disturbing was that, in effect, I had become Daisy's only friend – the one person who didn't treat her like shit, in her own words. She found that difficult. "You don't give up, do you?" "No I don't." She wouldn't be the only person to say those exact words. At the end of her second year, she took a placement at her own university in the microbiology labs. I had convinced her to take accommodation on campus, that was accessible for her as a recently diagnosed autistic person. The diagnosis had come through. Her mother had been helpful; her dad would "never know," because he saw autism as a form of laziness.

However, when Daisy and her mum came to move her stuff into the new accommodation we had, after many painful hours, managed to arrange, it was a disaster. It was filthy, there was rotting pizza in the oven, there was a wasp's nest underneath the sink. It was incredibly unsafe. Daisy needed things to be clean and under her control. She had a huge meltdown. Her mum was, like me, incensed, but Daisy forbade her – or me – from lodging any complaints.

In the end, I didn't get to speak to Daisy's mother, but restitution *was* paid to Daisy for not accepting the accommodation. This was serious. The trust was gone – not so much in me, but in the idea that fighting for anything was worth it. She started her placement, commuting from home for about five hours a day.

She wasn't sleeping, she wasn't eating, she wasn't communicating (much) with the other people at her placement. But despite all that, she flourished. She loved the lab work, though she never stopped complaining about her supervisors, making me laugh as she did so. She wasn't coping, but the work gave her life. It was so frustrating because the accommodations office had clearly let her down. But I could not raise a concern about it. This is what she wanted to do. I was caught between the devil and the deep blue sea.

Cut to me, later that day, when I was on the phone to her university's disability service and just cried to someone there. There was nothing they could do either – not without the student's request and consent. It was unfair, painfully so. But what could I do?

At one point, I confronted her with it: "What do you need me to do? I'm trying to help, I'm doing what I can, but you always say that you're fine when you're clearly not. What am I doing wrong?" She said, "Just do what you've been doing. I don't need help. I don't want help. I just want someone to shoot the shit with, every week." That's true. That was the limit of what she was willing to accept.

She'd call me "materino" whenever we'd talk. I was always happy to see her. Yes, her lecturers kept on being terrible, other students were pricks and travel was atrocious. But in her final year, she moved to a studio flat in town where she at least had her own space. She was clearly heading towards a first. Her supervisor on the placement told her she could go straight to a PhD. When Daisy shared the paper she was part of creating, I was so proud of her. She struggled to take that praise, deflecting the positive feedback, but it did make a difference. She started applying for positions, even getting interviews, but as far as I know, she hasn't landed a position yet.

In her final year, I helped her with the readability of her essays. She is the kind of autistic who's hyper-precise in her descriptions to the point where neurotypicals no longer focus on what she has to say. Her sentences were far longer than legible, even in academic English. As a teacher of English for Academic Purposes, I was all too happy to help.

She got a first. She actually fucking did it. I always knew, even if she didn't. She didn't allow me to come to her graduation, because she didn't want her father finding out she was talking to a strange man, even if he was gay. He also still doesn't know she's autistic. But my God, I am still so proud of her. The week before, her messages about feeling suicidal were getting more regular.

We stayed in touch, her sending me messages now and then while she continued to work at her (unpaid) university placement over the summer. When funding ran out, I asked her to request transition mentoring hours, in order to continue working together, which she didn't quite appreciate. Because Daisy had no friends, the relationship she had with me was the closest thing to friendship she had. But it wasn't friendship. Not at all. Like I said, something like a friendship will always develop, but a friendship it is not. Nor should it be. I am not their friend; I work for these students. When I share things about my life, that is because I am unmasking for their benefit. For Daisy, though, it felt like a betrayal.

"Do you only care about money?"

Since she doesn't pay me, and I don't accept students paying me out of pocket, I definitely don't want *her* money. But still, that was meant to hurt me. It also misunderstood my role on a basic level.

In September 2024, I was on my way to a friend's wedding and Daisy messaged me. She said that she realised she was not going to die because that would mean the book you're reading now would not have a happy ending. Whether that was true or not, I don't know. But whatever it was, it was not healthy.

I told my partner. He was firm. I agreed.

I blocked Daisy on my phone and messaged my boss at Bridge, Amanda. I told her everything. I said I wasn't helping, but instead was facilitating Daisy's anxieties about abandonment. This could not continue, in Daisy's best interest. Amanda is now in charge of Daisy's hours. She says Daisy will come when she's ready.

Be that as it may, I hope she's well. I hope she's alive. I hope that she's going to be able to break out of her isolation. She isn't alone. There's a world out there. When I introduced her to Zoey, they were the first other student at her university she had actually spoken to. This was during her third year. Zoey offered to stay in touch. Daisy never took them up on their offer. But Daisy did go out of her comfort zone a few times. She was part of a panel on making the university more accessible to autistic people. She went to the Disability Action Committee once and enjoyed it. She got her degree, and her name is out there now as a co-author on important microbiology research. She's got what it takes. I am happy that I was able to lay out a possible, potential future. What she decides to make of that is up to her. Finally, she is the one in control of her own life and destiny. I hope I at least convinced her that she's unique, hilarious and has the makings of a wonderful friend. I just couldn't – shouldn't – be that friend for her.

9
Zoey

Zoey had recently changed their name when I started working with them. They're AMAB non-binary – so, non-binary, assigned male at birth. At a university with a high focus on engineering, maths and sciences, they were studying French and Russian. I didn't know – still don't know! – a word of Russian, but I've studied French before, even teaching the language as a personal tutor. Of course, my knowledge of teaching English as a foreign language and doing an English degree meant I had quite the grounding in linguistics and translation, the last of which was the main focus of Zoey's degree.

Zoey's from a working-class family, living mainly with their dad and sister. When it comes to admin, they've had their act together from the start. When we started working together, the first issue was the university taking a massive payment for housing out in one go. That was, obviously, tricky – they now had £0.00 to live on in the short term. Zoey, pale with fear, told me they would survive, though, "because freezers exist", and they'd done enough cooking to last them well into winter. We ended up sorting out the overpayment with the admin team, but it wasn't easy.

Then, presentation skills. Zoey had it in their disability accessibility plan that presentations would be allowed via recorded video or audio, due to the anxiety that comes with presenting.

I get that: I only got over my stage fright by continually throwing myself at largely apathetic comedy audiences for over a decade. I now actively enjoy standing and talking in front of tonnes of people. I didn't use to, but things can change. I went through that baptism of fire; Zoey shouldn't have to, just to pass a languages degree.

Zoey met with one of their lecturers, who was less than charmed with their disability access plan. 'Can't you just do the thing, like everyone else?' No. That's the point. It was very difficult to make someone who believes they are being fair to all their students understand that by **not** giving certain people 'special treatment', they are, in fact, discriminating against them. This is rough for non-disabled people. Whenever we, as disabled people, talk about disability rights, we need to teach those without our lived experience about the social model. This model understands that being disabled is not something inherently wrong with *our* bodies, but that disabling certain people and enabling others is based on choices made by society. These are not so much individual choices (unless you're Elon Musk) but cultural ones, habits dripping into social life through centuries of unthinking repetition – *'this is just how it's done!'.*

As disabled people, we know that when arguing with non-disabled (or, rather, not-YET-disabled) people, there is no middle ground when it comes to accessibility. Mainstream education provision assumes that everyone is equally enabled and disabled people just have to work a little bit harder. Often, when arguing about these basic provisions, organisations will say: "well, we *could* provide these adjustments, but it has to come from *both* sides." As advocates, we cannot accept this fake compromise. It presumes that disabled people want special treatment – participation trophies – rather than actually receive the same treatment as everyone else. This is false, and advocates have to be obvious about this: an autistic person is *already* making adjustments for everyone else, simply by being in a space where neurotypical norms hold sway.

The problems we face go as deep as the very language that disability legislation is written in: 'reasonable adjustments'. Adjustments – that's fine – but reasonable to whom, exactly? For a mainstream employer or education provider, ALL adjustments tend to be unreasonable. As advocates, we need to highlight the choices these organisations are already making, simply by adhering to the status quo.

In the end, Zoey was allowed to film their presentations, as well as give a one-on-one presentation with a member of staff. This wasn't fun; the lecturer's "there, that wasn't so bad, was it?" wasn't fun either. But they did it. They got through first year.

In order to afford housing, Zoey needed to pay their own way, as they had been doing for several years before they went to uni. They were working at a large multinational fast-food brand. And yes, there were plenty of examples of exclusion and patronising attitudes from customers and fellow staff, but, fundamentally, Zoey felt at home, even making it to a supervisory role.

However, there are huge inequalities between autistic people who attend university. Some have parents who can afford to pay their tuition, so they don't have debts. Some even buy them a flat in town at great expense so that their child can study. I didn't work with any of those students. My students were more or less living off their student loans, which, from 2021 to 2024 started representing less and less opportunity to actually survive. Working alongside uni is tough. It requires yet more adaptation to a neurotypical workplace, on top of the already exhausting daily stress of being in a highly neurotypical environment. I was fired from and failed interviews multiple times during my student years. Each of them was as humiliating as the next. Zoey, though, has managed to stick it out.

Doing a languages degree, Zoey needed to do a year abroad in a country where their chosen language is spoken. For them, that's French and Russian. The first one was easy, but during Zoey's first year, Russia's full-scale invasion of Ukraine began. The only place where it might have been slightly safe for an autistic, non-binary, gay student to learn Russian would have been Kyiv, but for obvious reasons, that was no longer applicable. I was firm: "you're *not* going to Russia." They agreed. After long deliberation, the university's study abroad team agreed that Zoey was to go to France, for a full year. I would support them in their preparation, including with public speaking, as well as finding the right university which would provide equivalent disability support.

During second year, we continued meeting, sometimes face to face, in order to prepare for the year abroad. Zoey told me they were specialising in autism and neurodiversity for an elective course in the teaching of English as a Foreign Language, as well as becoming part of their university's disability action collective, a group of students arguing for appropriate treatment of disabled students and staff. They were ticking all the boxes when it came to preparing for university abroad. I told them repeatedly that I'd be there and that they were going to get through this. They weren't alone.

I told Zoey about my experience on the Erasmus programme, moving from Holland to Sussex University in Brighton. But I also highlighted the very real difficulties that I encountered, as well as the fact that not every country is as "good" for disabled people as the UK (and those quotation marks are doing a *lot* of heavy lifting). I'm Dutch and I know that the difference in the narrative in the UK is profound compared to the Netherlands. Disabled activism, specifically disabled Left activism, is a meaningful force in the UK. In Holland, not so much. France, where Zoey was going, not so much either. As an activist, I meet a lot of autistic people from across the world. France is not the best place in the world to be autistic, shall we say. The focus on 'so-called treatment' for autistic people has moved from initially blaming mothers for their perceived coldness – Bruno Bettelheim's 'refrigerator mothers' – to ABA. From the frying pan into the fire. I told staff at Zoey's university about my concerns, and they got the promise that their support in France would be identical. In short, the UK's disability provision is obviously atrocious. The rest of the world is, in many ways, simply worse.

We both know where this is going. When they went to France, despite promises, there was nothing. The lecturers weren't aware that Zoey was autistic or even what that meant. Zoey's lectures weren't recorded; the lectures were passive, old-fashioned affairs in large, echoey theatres, from unbothered lecturers. The student housing was cold and inhospitable, as were the locals. By December, things were going badly. I could see it over the increasingly frequent Zoom calls we had. Zoey was even paler than usual, a scraggly, unkempt beard hiding the fact that they weren't eating, since life was far more expensive there than expected.

The disability service? Nowhere to be seen, neither from their home university nor in France. Zoey needed to battle for every scrap, which would then be denied, either explicitly or by omission and neglect. All they'd asked for was consistency. The only thing that was consistent was meeting with me – surely Zoey's home university wasn't saying this was what consistency meant?

About ten days before Christmas, I got a text from Zoey: "Can you please call?" I had time. We did. They'd gone in for their first exam of the week, only to find out that they were never notified about a change in dates to their exams. Despite studying hard this week, without the usual support, they simply missed all their exams. They had not left their room for the previous week; they'd been self-harming. "You're going home," I said. They did.

Back in England, the first few weeks were just about recuperating. Things were not great, but they were safe. They, thankfully, decided not to go back to work immediately.

The university did not help. They treated Zoey as if they were simply refusing to go back to France. As if they couldn't be bothered. As if what happened hadn't happened. We met online with a few members of staff responsible for the study abroad year. Zoey wanted to know how the university was going to support them. The university instead proposed that Zoey somehow recoup the learning they lost by 'not attending' the year abroad, for instance, by visiting an online language school – paid for with their own money. If we weren't happy about it, Zoey could raise a complaint.

They were pretty defeated. Angry, too. They went back to work while going through the university complaints department. The complaint was not upheld since this was not a case where the policies weren't upheld by an individual member of staff. No, the policy itself is the problem in how it treats disabled students, but a complaint can never be about that. When students decide to complain about inadequate, non-existent or abusive conditions, this is the way these things tend to go. The UK has some of the best disability legislation in the world. It also has some of the worst adherence *to* that legislation. Unless government bodies, businesses and organisations actually fear the law on the books, nothing will change (see the work of autistic legal scholar Yo Dunn). The current system is working perfectly well – against the bodies of the disabled (see *Crippled* by Frances Ryan).

Fourth year started; things seemed to be better. But only a few weeks in, Zoey messaged me in a state of high distress. Their work had been flagged as created by generative AI. My boss, Amanda, and I calmed Zoey down, but we were disturbed by this. The day before, we'd been contacted by Zoey's university, which asked us if they were attending classes and accessing support. They were. The week after, I met with Zoey, Zoey's course leader, their study skills tutor and a member of staff from the department.

What Zoey had done was write an essay on a topic of their choosing (Zoey's choice: linguistics) that they should have been getting support with from the university in France – which they left in December 2023 – and from their home university, none of whose staff members are linguists. Therefore, Zoey used ChatGPT to help provide a structure for a paper on sociolinguistics, historical linguistics and phonology. But that wasn't the problem. This was not a case where an algorithm used to check for plagiarism found any. We found out that Zoey's paper was read by a human being, who just 'felt' that Zoey's paper had been written by AI.

Now, autistic people do **not** write 'like AI'; in fact, we are highly creative, even innovative with our language use. However, when we write for academic purposes, we write for a particular audience (neurotypicals) with a particular goal (getting a passing grade for a university course). For neurotypical readers, it doesn't really seem to matter *how* we write. Even in our writing, even anonymised, we still face accusations of being 'not real'. This is going to be a serious problem.

A friend of mine's sibling had their paper marked for potential generative AI use. It wasn't written with generative AI. Another paper, which *was* written by generative AI, was *not* marked for plagiarism. This is particularly egregious, since generative AI simply *is* plagiarism. Gen AI is not intelligence. It's an aggregate, stealing from every piece of text ever uploaded onto the internet. It is a massive data set of stolen content.

If neurotypical marking officers read autistic people's writing as plagiarised while allowing AI-generated writing through, then there is a serious problem with how AI usage is dealt with in higher education. The university staff members said to Zoey that there had been a number of "false flags" so far this year. It wouldn't surprise Zoey, they said, if the vast majority of those flags were autistic students, none of whom had plagiarised. Of course, a few days after the meeting, Zoey's plagiarism enquiry was dismissed as an example of a "false flag".

Zoey will finish university this year, probably with a very high grade. They are committed to disability and queer rights, and social justice. I think they're going to make an absolute nuisance of themselves over the next few years. I'm ready with the popcorn.

10
Stephen

When I met Stephen, he was not in town. Instead, he was with his girlfriend in Oxford, where I used to live as well. He hadn't been to uni for weeks – months. He was studying product design at a university closer to me than to the town I used to live in and things were not going well for him. Like Daisy, he was also undiagnosed at this point. We started talking, mostly through jokes. We made each other laugh – big time.

He was born and brought up on the Gold Coast. I'd been to Australia in 1999 and I have a deep emotional connection to the place, including being able to do an incredibly accurate set of Australian accents – from hard Bogan to Melburnian deconstructed latte-liker, from Steve Irwin to Kylie Minogue and Troye Sivan.

He's tall, like me, and also an immigrant to the UK. He moved from Australia after traumatic school years, living with a family member who didn't value him. Off his own back, he worked to get himself qualifications, since he left Australia without any. He studied for his A-levels in the North of England, then moved down to the South West for uni. In the North of England, he met his now partner. They stuck together like glue, to the point where Stephen's first year at uni without her was exhausting. He didn't connect with anyone, just wanting – needing – to be with her. He somehow passed first year, by virtue of his capacity in maths.

> *"I haven't attended any classes since the first few weeks."*
> "What caused that?"
> *"I mean – fuck! – we were expected to use this fucking wind tunnel to test our model. It was so loud. It was awful. I was in so much pain."*
> "Do you know that I've been sent your way by the **name of uni redacted** disability service?"
> *"I kinda guessed."*
> "And that I'm an autistic mentor, for autistic people."
> *"Yeah, about that."*

He had been in and out of children's and adolescent mental health care as a teenager in Australia. He'd been on and off medication, struggling mightily. Now, his father was chronically ill. His father is English, from the North West, his mother is from the Baltic states. Most of his family is ridiculously far away. Like for me, England was a lifeline for Stephen – many autistic people leave the country they were born in to try to make a life for themselves abroad. I did. But after all his effort, Stephen was hitting brick walls.

> *"I just, can't. I can't get through this block. I just don't have the capacity."*
> "Do you self-medicate?"
> *"What do you mean?"*
> "Alcohol, drugs, self-harm, handball?"
> *"Not the handball. But the first two, yes. It calms the anxiety."*

Again, relatable content. I have been sober since 2012, when I was using alcohol in order to fall asleep. That was not a good time for me. It's always painful to see that others are using drugs and alcohol to cope with unbearable situations. When it comes to autistic people and drug and alcohol use – or other forms of self-harm like eating disorders – what matters is that we understand the substance abuse not as a problem in and of itself. We use substances in order to cope with something else in life. For Stephen, school was what caused his issues with alcohol and drugs.

I told him that his alcohol use wasn't helping the anxiety (for now, I avoided the terms 'meltdown' and 'overload'). He should consider really cutting down, preferably to zero. As for marijuana, that was different. Some autistic people use weed and hash and it does them good – my best friend, for instance. The only thing I made them promise was not to smoke it with tobacco but to vaporise the stuff or make edibles. Tobacco is far more directly harmful. But for others, especially those with schizophrenia in the family, weed is a terrible idea, raising their likelihood of psychotic episodes dramatically. If those people are using weed, that's self-harm. They aren't trying to get high; they're trying to destroy themselves. One other mentee is in this exact situation – his friends have supported him, and he has now stopped using entirely.

I told Stephen to be mindful of how he was using marijuana, to change from smoking to vaporising or edibles, and to check in with himself. He should want to get high *because* he wants to get high, rather than as a crutch, because he using it to be functional will only exacerbate his anxiety ("paranoia is a problem, yeah") and his other health issues, like IBS.

Self-harm because we want to be functional is a weird concept for anyone who hasn't experienced this themselves. Basically, when you're an autistic child and you're burned out from the stress of existing in a neurotypical world, we are taught/teach ourselves to mete out punishment towards ourselves. I used to bite myself, pinch my skin, and, when I was older, get into fights because I wanted to be punished for not being normal. My rage at myself for not being normal is what caused me a meltdown so severe I found myself in hospital in 2012. As stated before, Dutch psychiatry's answer? Drugs. Tonnes of 'em. Until very recently, when my body screamed for rest in the face of deadlines, I watched porn for hours, kicking myself in the cerebellum to give myself enough energy to just finish the thing. Stephen was doing the very same thing – to no avail, it seemed.

> "Are you feeling safe around yourself?"
> "Yeah, I kinda do. But I'm more worried for my girlfriend."

Stephen's girlfriend has a chronic illness *and* was doing a very intense science degree at Oxford. He felt a huge level of responsibility towards her, trying his best to hide his anxiety and to use drugs when she was not in the student lodgings they now shared. He wasn't really leaving the house much except for shopping and the very basics, so he'd be screaming at himself for not getting work done on his degree, not being able to clean and cook for his girlfriend and just getting stoned instead. It was a very obvious vicious cycle.

> "Do you still enjoy your degree."
> "No. I really don't."

That was the most direct Stephen had been about his feelings. Like others I write about here, Stephen was struggling with alexithymia, figuring out how exactly he was feeling and simply not knowing until later. I explained that this was pretty fundamental to autism.

> "Do you want to know what I think?"
> "…Yeah?"
> "I think you need a break."
> "But I just had a break! I haven't done much of anything these past few months."

I know what that's like too. During my MA, not long after my conversation with my own mentor, the strain of my MA started wearing me down. I started sleeping more and more and becoming less and less functional. By Christmas, I was no longer coping on any level. I couldn't read, I couldn't think, I couldn't produce anything. I tried to force myself to get work done, but simply couldn't. In January 2014, I spoke to my course leader. He could see what was going on. Together, we decided I should go on study leave. Yes, another one. I had already taken an extra year to finish my undergrad, when I wasn't allowed to graduate for the sake of my mental health, back in 2012. The staff didn't believe it was safe for me to graduate and take up my place at UCL, so I stuck around for another year. This time, however, it took me two full years to recover, whereas in 2012–2013, I frankly hadn't. Why? Drugs. I was prescribed a *lovely* cocktail of medication – especially the clonazepam – that I was only able to withdraw from with help from a private psychotherapist in 2015. She was a complete hero, especially since she was no longer charging me for attending. Rachel Pollard saved my life; she really did. I only started to be able to put her advice into practice years later, when I was no longer a student. With this experience, I knew that Stephen had no choice.

> "I do think you need time. Take the rest of this year. Not just this term. You need time to heal."

He wasn't happy to hear that, but he could see where I was coming from. He got a bit emotional, too. But he agreed. Next time, his girlfriend joined. She was just out of reach of the camera. He told her everything. She agreed immediately. It was time for Stephen to heal. We got in touch with the university, had a meeting and it was settled. Stephen was going on an official interruption.

Since the university, rather than the DSA, was paying for mentoring, I was able to continue, especially since Stephen told them how much working with me was helping him. We kept on meeting; he quit drinking and smoking weed. Having thought about it, he agreed that, yes, he was autistic. He just didn't have the diagnostic statements from when he was a teenager. Enter Stephen's mother, who got us an email address for his previous psychiatrist. Together, we wrote emails and even made phone calls to Australia to retrieve his documentation. In it, the word *'autism?'* was circled. This, I believed, was more than good enough. We got in touch with his university and the NHS, who still needed to diagnose him internally. He started that process.

In January 2022, I got a text from Stephen that said: "Hey Jorik, I started a course on autism!" Knowing what most courses on autism looked like, I held fire: "that's great! What is it based on? Is it made by autistic people?" A few weeks before, I'd been seeing ads on Instagram, advertising Autism Level 2 courses. They were also priced at £0.00, as stated in the ad, which isn't that great if you're an autistic person, part of whose income derives from educating on autism. I decided to do some digging, getting in touch with the course provider. Apparently, they were linked to Further Education colleges around the country, which would assess the course (read: punch in numbers onto a spreadsheet from a multiple-choice exam and print a certificate for the learner) but had absolutely no control over the content. Well, if not them, who did?

After a couple of phone calls, I found out that the course provider based its work on a book written by a non-autistic author, without contributions from the autistic community. But, they assured me, the content was scientifically tested and adhered to the latest science.

I know that story. ABA providers always use their purported scientific undergirding as a veil to cover up the inherent abusive nature of these programmes, whether or not any individual provider believes they are abusing people. It's a beautifully constructed ideological cover-up. The people responsible don't intend to harm disabled people; disabled people are just **so** disabled that even the best, most scientifically rigorous attempts at curing them don't work out after all. Ah well. But that's not the point. The point is to continue providing conversion therapy, which traumatises those who undergo it, seeking mental healthcare, for which the only answer is more conversion therapy! It's an amazing example of a pyramid scheme, exploiting its own market and resources cyclically, extracting money from autistic people's suffering. In a world that has no alternative for autistic people (like the United States), it's a magic money tree.

I'm obviously being facetious. The outcomes of conversion therapy are simple: trauma and death. Despite ABA's defenders using different brand names and providers, covered with the veil of good intentions, our lives are still what are being bought and sold. More on this in *Feeling Fast and Slow*, of course.

What was Stephen's course teaching, then? He sent me a scan of his textbook. Despite a quick nod to the neurodiversity movement in the coursebook's most recent edition, the course taught PBS – positive behaviour support – the *very English*, passive-aggressive variant of ABA I spoke about in the introduction. Fuck. The book was teaching that autism is based, fundamentally, *on* misbehaviour. If autistic people decided to behave in line with neurotypicals, they would be, in Lovaas' words, "indistinguishable" from their neurotypical peers. Stephen did *not* need that, especially when he was just trying to figure himself out. To use the Instagram algorithm to particularly advertise these materials to autistic people trying to find out who they were was, frankly disgusting. Worse, Stephen found out that if he decided to leave the course without finishing it, he would be liable for the full cost: £850. "I don't have that kind of money!" Of course he didn't, otherwise he wouldn't have chosen a free course advertised to him on Instagram because of his disability. Businesses are very happy to take advantage of disabled people, as evidenced by Stephanie Sterling's YouTube series on the ableism of microtransactions in video games. In those episodes, they show that online gaming companies seek to use 'free-to-play' models that allow gamers to buy in-game content or progression tools, sometimes at the cost of thousands. Autistic people are usually exhausted from spending time in the neurotypical world, which affects our impulse control. Stephen wasn't a gambler, but he was definitely a mark, used by this company to either get the government to pay for a course in conversion therapy that Stephen would complete or have him drop out and pay £850. No matter what happened, the provider got paid. Again, this is how capitalism works. Disabled people are not the target audience; we are the raw materials for capitalist extraction.

I got in touch first with the local college, who were horrified to hear of its content. I then had several phone calls with very apologetic members of staff. I stated my case early and did not change: only a full rewrite by a diverse team of autistic writers would resolve this. Before that, Stephen should be allowed to leave the course without paying for it. I raised a complaint about the debt trap Stephen was put in, as well as a complaint about advertising conversion therapy to disabled people using social media. I made those complaints in early 2022. As of November 2024, I have yet to hear back from this company. Stephen was allowed to leave the course at no financial cost to him, which was my main concern.

As for the course materials, I spent several hours across 2023 assessing both the course materials and the course outline from the overarching organisation for Further Education colleges across the UK. Both were suffused with conversion therapy practices, like the modules from my first mentoring company. Not good. I was paid for my time, but none of the issues I raised were taken on board, since no other readers had highlighted any problems with it, nor was it outside the mainstream of psychological discourse on autistic people. Yeah, I know, that's the problem. We need to change the discourse from the ground up, as well as top-down. As stated before, the Disabilities and Equalities Acts 2010 are some of the best pieces of legislation against discrimination in the world, but adherence to these laws is negligible, especially within the disability sphere. The fight goes on, clearly.

As for Stephen, he started meeting up with autistic people near him in Oxford. He realised he'd fallen out of love with his subject – he now wanted to be a maths teacher. After he'd found out I was a personal tutor, he wanted to know more, so I told him. I advised him to tutor maths to other autistic people. This gave him more energy than he'd ever got from his degree. By late spring, he told me he wanted to drop out to take a degree in maths education via the Open University. We haven't really spoken since, because if students want to contact me after leaving university, they can, but I won't initiate that contact. As far as I know, he is still doing his degree and enjoying life as a newly married man, understanding himself more than he ever did before. He opened up to himself over the year I worked with him. I'm massively proud of Stephen, and I hope he can one day see how much he's achieved.

11
Nik

Nik's details were sent my way in the spring of 2023. We met online the very same evening. He'd not been in a good way, to say the least. He was a second-year engineering student and had just got home from the hospital after an overnight sectioning after a suicide attempt. Things were bad. His girlfriend had broken up with him. Their relationship had been platonic and nearly all online, but that didn't matter. His emotional connection to her was real in a way that she didn't feel at all. He was already not on top of his work this term. His younger brother was not yet free from throat cancer and he, as the eldest son now in uni, away from London where he grew up, was not coping. He'd also just been blackmailed. Via social media, he was approached by a woman he didn't know, for cam sex. Then he was blackmailed.

This happens a lot. The internet has previously seen famous people have online sex with someone they haven't met, then blackmail them with the threat of releasing the video to the public. A comedian I've gigged with suffered this a few years ago and it didn't harm his career. A gay Tory MP fell victim to a scam like this only last year. It did harm his. In the UK, Black and Asian young men are more likely to fall victim to this ploy, due to expectations around masculinity and sexual norms. Nik is short for Nikesh and his parents are both Indian immigrants, one Muslim, one Hindu.

They'd had to fight the Home Office at one point; they were supposed to be deported. They now have permanent leave to remain, but as an immigrant, you will never feel safe from deportation, even with supposed assurances to the contrary. Nik was the one who needed to perform, he felt. Instead, he couldn't concentrate on anything.

The vast majority of people diagnosed with autism in this country are still white. This is odd, since race isn't a biological category and autistic people are just as likely to exist within every ethnicity. Instead, blame is often cast on a lack of disability awareness **within** these communities rather than looking inwards. Autism doesn't have a **look**. But there is a reason why I was diagnosed at eight years old in the mid-1990s and others won't have been. I was a cis boy, I was a little gay, I wore glasses, I spoke with an annoying voice about dinosaurs and I was, crucially, white. The visual media made about autistic people usually highlights white autistics – with the laudable counter-example of Jerry Rothwell's *The Reason I Jump* (2021). With Nik, there was a lot of work to do initially.

First, he needed to stabilise. I asked if he needed a study break. He didn't, not right now. I asked if he was comfortable in his student house. He was. The people he lived with were incredibly supportive. In fact, the hospitalisation had shunted him out of his creative block. He ended up doing six months' worth of coursework in two or three weeks. I kept a close eye on him. He could be in a state where he was running before he could walk. I know from bitter experience what that feels like. He wanted to get back to studying, but the disability service at his uni hadn't managed to get him the support he needed. Something was different with me, though. Despite having been diagnosed years ago, he hadn't worked with another autistic adult before, not like this. Like with Brandon, the student population at his university was surprisingly neurotypical.

I was there, I was supportive. We booked body-doubling sessions, where I did admin or did the washing up while he worked on engineering problems. He wanted to make aeroplanes, so he did a lot of complex maths and physics to facilitate that. My dyscalculic ass couldn't be of much help to him, but I could for language. Despite growing up in East London, he didn't speak English until he went to school, his parents raising him at first in Hindi/Urdu. Grammar and collocations were his weak points, so he talked me through his written coursework and I provided feedback. This sounds like plagiarism, stated like this, but in reality, this is how students are expected to work. Students are expected to ask for feedback from their peer group and collaborate, understanding the course materials collectively. Autistic people are less likely to fall into friendship groups where this process occurs automatically, so we often struggle alone. To have a mentor is to have a chance to undo this particular social consequence of being disabled in a neurotypical environment.

One thing was still there, though, bubbling away in the background: the fear of blackmail. The police said they couldn't do anything besides telling him not to pay, block the scammer from accessing his social media and report the scammer's phone number as spam. Usually, the problem will just go away. As I told Nik, these organisations are run by syndicates situated in the Global South – primarily West Africa and South-East Asia, some in Russia. In practice, what they do is not that different from how companies work in the Global North. Their staff go to work in what is functionally a call centre, like I did in 2008 when I worked for a multinational bank in the credit department. It was my job to tell people to pay off their loans after payments were missed. What Nik experienced was just someone in a call centre doing a job. He wasn't personally singled out. He was vulnerable and the scammers pounced. Disabled people therefore suffer more from this particular financial carnivory.

> "It's not that. I don't want any of my friends to see that, that video. Especially not my female friends."

Here I had a choice to make. I could do what neurotypical support workers would be advised to do and steer away from the topic or, of course say: "that must be so hard for you".

Instead, I was direct.

> "Nik, I'm a gay in my thirties. I've had cam sex with people. My dick will be somewhere on the internet. That's fine. Because of how relationships have changed, particularly during the pandemic, our entire generation will have nudes somewhere online. That's okay."
> *"But my friends, the ones who are girls-"*
> "What, they'll be shocked that you masturbate? Of course not! Simply tell them if it ever happens. They'll be fine. They'd be more upset if you'd never wanked before."

That was the reality check Nik needed. Yes, it's awkward to talk about sex with mentees. I don't particularly enjoy doing so. But who else are they going to open up to? Nik is a young autistic man. Simply by having sexual thoughts and feelings, he will already be seen by wider society as a bit gross. I tried dating women when I was closeted. It didn't work for me. My partner is bisexual and he's still struck by the ease with which he was dismissed and ridiculed by girls he found attractive back when he was in his teens. We were both ashamed – and shamed – of having sexual desires to begin with.

Nik ended up passing all his modules in a month-long rush of hyperfocus. He got into third year. We worked together closely for a module connected to economics, preparing the engineering students for work in the private sector. Nik hadn't done much economics, but he decided he wanted to research a company in India that sold educational materials online, which had grown hugely during the pandemic and was accused of conspiring with India's far-right Modi government to increase its value for the sake of shareholders.

Nik had been in India, visiting family and, in his own words, "avoiding arranged marriage proposals" in the summer of 2023. He hadn't been since he was a small child. He therefore didn't know many of his relatives. It was useful for him, learning what it's like to spend time in another country, another culture, in which his own position wasn't certain either. I knew from reading the news and keeping up to date that Modi's India was not a safe place for someone like Nik. Islamophobia is rife under Modi's Hindu nationalist BJP party. India is also the country with the largest minority Muslim population in the world: 200 million people out of India's total of 1.4 billion.

With this knowledge, we got into a proper rabbit hole together, researching English-language Indian media for references to this particular company. The story we found was astounding. My job was to share how to do research in the humanities and social sciences and keep him on track. He got a first for the course.

Usually, in Nik's integrated master's course, the third year would be a professional placement. For the previous reasons, Nik had not been able to find a placement, which, like Marcus, really demotivated him. This time, it was different. Without any help from his university, he spent over 150 hours just doing job interviews and cognitive and psychometric tests, all of which he failed because he is autistic. That does not include the time spent applying for placements, sending emails and writing cover letters. The job application process has become less and less accessible over the decades. Autistic people are now the most likely group of disabled people to be unemployed in the United Kingdom. That isn't because we've suddenly become incapable; that is because of very specific choices made by systems of human resource management, intentionally or not, excluding us from the workplace. I told Nik this, but he was going to go for it all the same.

Several months into his quest, he got to the final round with about four companies hiring for placement students. He failed those too. Then, out of nowhere, Nik calls me to tell me he's got a placement. How? It was the one company small enough not to use an HR system. I was so proud of him. Blood, sweat and tears, and he'd finally got something.

However, the company required a police check for all its applicants. If you've seen those, you need to tick a box if you've spent more than a month in a country other than the UK. Nik had – that summer, in India. He was incandescent with rage at himself. I talked him down. It was going to be alright. When I started teaching, I needed to provide a police check from the Dutch police, having lived in the Netherlands before I immigrated. He needed to go down to London to chat with the Indian consulate. We had a meeting to contact the consulate and organise the trip. He got the police check within weeks. If he hadn't had that, he couldn't have started his placement in early summer.

He is now at that placement, doing what he loves. Since we started working together, he's developed as a human being. He's kinder to himself and has learned that being autistic isn't something to be ashamed of. He has visited the Autwell group and loved it. After all this time, things are going Nik's way and I look forward to continuing to support him during his MSc.

12
Noah

Another mentee of mine, Noah, asked to speak to me face to face in 2023. What had happened? He wanted to talk about his sexuality. I was ready: "okay, so you would like to talk about dating other guys?" No, apparently not. "Oh!" In reality, Noah had not done any uni work for months on end. The reason was that he procrastinated, got bored, horny and watched porn. But because he was watching women, he fell into a cycle of blaming himself for being sexist and not allowing himself to do any work as punishment. That punishment impulse is actually common in autistic people.

In 2019, at Autscape, I asked the speaker (and friend) Leneh Buckle about her research into autistic inertia. What about punishing oneself *for* inertia? She hadn't heard of this particular reaction before. But, my God, is it common. We've already encountered several students who show this exact response.

With Noah, it's complicated. He has plenty of female friends and massively respects women. He'd describe himself as a feminist, especially now. So, in mid-2023, Noah and I kept on talking about his mental health and his sexual needs. Having a healthy relationship with sex is really important, especially if you *want* to have sex but *haven't* yet.

Enter, once again, incel culture. Autistic men who are attracted to women – they may be queer in ways they don't yet account for or, like me in my early twenties, want to have a shot at being *'normal'* – are routinely mocked for being nerdy and weird, unattractive, not masculine. Even gay men, whose mainstream beauty standards don't include autistic people, can be equally exclusionary. Because of who we are, we are pushed to the margins of masculinity. Manosphere influencers are willing to offer this privilege back to us, at a cost.

For Noah, that cost was watching porn, then obsessively watching no-fap influencers on YouTube. The name is stupid, of course, referring to an online euphemism for masturbation. Noah watched these men, desperately trying to train himself not to masturbate, since it apparently damages one's masculine energy. He needed to punish himself for masturbating, not just because it was non-masculine but also because it was inherently sexist.

This is, needless to say, bullshit. As I state in *Feeling Fast and Slow*, the porn and sex work industries are used as a metaphor for patriarchy – women's bodies exploited for profit. But in practice, it just doesn't work like that. People have jobs. For many, including women, sex work is no more exploitative than working in a call centre or at McDonald's. Quite a few autistic women do sex work, since it allows them to take care of themselves and their bodies (especially women who have chronic illnesses), is less socially intensive than working in an office, and is better paid than retail or catering. Is working in a call centre less exploitative than being an independent sex worker?

Secondly, Noah was wrong about masturbation. It *is* healthy, normal, and does not say anything about one's masculinity.

I shared a video with him from an American queer YouTuber who talks about masturbation and healthy masculinities. This was an eye-opener for Noah, not just because the dude was practically naked while talking about the spiritual benefits of having a wank. But simply being told that he was sliding into a far-right manosphere rabbit hole and being shown the error of his ways, didn't fix his sense of worthlessness, or the notion that he's a bit creepy, that his desires were inappropriate and abusive, simply because he had them. He wouldn't be the only one, either. Several autistic boys and men I've spoken to have felt that they were somehow inherently rapey. I've felt like that.

That sounds like an absurd conclusion to come to, but that is what this kind of exclusionary thinking does. And no, it is not women who hold this in place: it's men. It's patriarchy. Patriarchy sets up idealised masculinities and, by insisting on sexual profligacy as inherently masculine, separates men into incels and chads. As for Noah, he believed that he, by nature, was disgusting and needed to be constrained. Many autistic men I've spoken to feel this way. The reality of the situation is, however, very different.

In 2021, the Supreme Court of the United Kingdom decided on a case brought by an autistic man with learning disabilities regarding whether he had the right to have sex with people. The High Court said yes; the Supreme Court said no. Not because he's learning disabled, as some might think. Instead, he was denied the right to sex due to his autism. Why? One of their *'expert'* witnesses was a behaviourist psychologist, who uses behaviour modification against autistic people. Apparently, what makes someone autistic is our innate lack of empathy and our incapacity to read body language. Therefore, autistic people do not understand consent.

Let that sink in for a second.

My first thought: *'Why then are we all in the kink scene?'* My partner and I are loosely connected to the queer kink community in Bristol. What is BDSM, if not collaborative stimming? Consent is **vital** for BDSM. As someone who takes a dominant role in kink scenes, my main job is to observe my partner very directly, listening to him, making sure he is enjoying himself. I am not in charge of the scene – he is. And if he is uncomfortable, I will end the scene immediately. With very few exceptions, everyone in the queer Bristol kink scene is neurospicy. That's *why* we're good at it: we are hugely aware of the other person's consent.

However, the Court ruled that autistic people *are* capable of indicating whether or not *they themselves* consent to sex.

Wow.

What about alexithymia, when autistic people struggle to express whether or not they feel good about something? What does that do to our capacity for informed consent in the moment? What about social pressure? What about the number of autistic people who are on the asexual spectrum, who feel the need to have sex in order to be *'normal'*? What about the fact that autistic people are *more*, not less, likely to be the victims of sexual assault and rape? I work with sexual violence prevention and trauma support organisations to make their provision more specific for neurodivergent people, in order to reduce harm to our community.

I really think this decision, which is now case law, is going to make our lives a lot worse over the next few years. I hope not, but we can't be sure. As long as autistic men and boys are seen as creepy, even rapey, by their peers, simply for experiencing sexual attraction; as long as autistic women and girls feel like heteronormative sex with less-than-savoury men will make them be counted as women; as long as autistic ace people are forced to present in hetero, cis and allosexual-normative ways, none of us are safe. These beliefs, held by mainstream neurotypical culture need to be questioned, queried and queered, which I do more of in *Feeling Fast and Slow*.

That is the reason I was honest with Nik about my penis likely being on the internet somewhere. That's why I told Noah that wanking was healthy.

Noah now has friends – real friends – at uni, as well as at home. All of them are autistic. Most, if not all of them, belong to the LGBTQIA+ alphabet mafia. Connecting to women as friends has been extremely healthy. Being friends with other men, having counter-examples of autistic queer masculinities, has been hugely beneficial for him too, whatever relationships – or none – Noah ever chooses to exist in. It will take time – a long time – to start really believing he is not a creep simply because he exists. But he's on his way. This year, he'll graduate.

13
Tim

When I started with Tim, he was very behind. Studying Games Design, at a university in Scotland, he'd had long periods of non-attendance at school. He and his twin brother were both autistic and both studied at the same university – Tim in third year, his twin in first. He really struggled with creative block, writer's block, he called it. It *kind of* is.

Autistic inertia is not the most well-known aspect of being autistic. Rather, our capacity to hyperfocus is far more culturally significant. But, pardon me for being a bit extreme here, I think we can understand it better when we push against diagnostic boundaries a little, seeing them (especially in neurodiversity) as the culturally defined and historically contingent deficit frames that they are. As an autistic activist, I have never met an autistic person without massive executive dysfunction issues. I have also never met an ADHDer without issues socialising, intense focus on what interests them, sensory issues and every other signifier of autism. I believe autism and ADHD are not words that describe distinct states of brains suffering from curable conditions. Instead, these are terms that describe a certain kind of person. That person is the same, depending on what diagnosticians choose to focus on, depending on the socio-cultural presentation of the person in front of them. ADHD is not "*cured*" by medication, nor is autism "*cured*" by behaviour modification "*therapy*". Sure, there is a possibility of an overlap in the way that a hypothetical autistic brain and a hypothetical ADHD brain process the world. But, so far, I'm sceptical. The medical system is very far from actually describing what goes on in the brain, so it's wise to take the diagnostic mainstream with a grain of salt. To be autistic is to be a certain kind of human being. It's a social, not a medical, category. This doesn't mean I embrace pseudoscience instead. Science is real, within a historical framework that helps us understand reality at this particular point in time. Until we have a "*completed* neuroscience" (which might never happen) we will just have to use scepticism and the welfare of the student to ascertain what benefits them the most.

When I told Tim about inertia, it was a new concept to him. He'd always conceived of himself as lazy and unbothered. He lives with his mother and twin brother in a small house in the suburbs of his university town. In the past, Tim struggled with OCD, leaving him stuck in his own room for months on end. Tim was embarrassed about this time, as if mental ill health was something to be ashamed of. I told him I wouldn't be. OCD is an anxiety disorder. It doesn't describe a kind of person, like autistic does. OCD is what's called ego-dystonic. It exists, like toothache, no matter the kind of person you are. OCD is a response to other things in the world that give someone distress. If anything, OCD is a healthy response to a traumatic environment. Checking things keeps us safe from accidents and cleanliness from infection. But it starts to become a problem when a person experiences distress from their own anxious thinking patterns. My argument is that no one can be distressed from **being** autistic, only from their environment treating them worse than other people. "I am autistic" is an identity-statement. OCD is not. It's curable, by finding adequate support and being kind to oneself.

I couldn't break through Tim's inertia, no matter how much he wanted to. I tried it myself; it doesn't work. When my brain is going at a million miles an hour, I need to rest. That's it. His mother found this difficult. For the past twenty years, all she'd heard was that she wasn't doing *enough* to make her sons actually do the things that they were supposed to do. The conversation was always about work ethic, structure and no longer being lazy. When I came in, saying the exact opposite, that took some getting used to. But she's there now. I spoke to her, back in 2023, over the phone. It was tough to hear one thing from every single professional she'd spoken to over her children's lives, and the exact opposite from me. I believe that autistic people aren't lazy. We are expected to work *more* than those around us. This is exhausting. We may have greater capacity to perceive the world sensorily, but we don't have greater bandwidth. We can't force ourselves into a world made for brains we don't possess. But even this is historically contingent. I like to use an example Hilary Mantel used in her 2017 Reith Lectures. Thomas Cromwell's London, in the sixteenth century, represented a vastly different sensory experience from London in the twenty-first century. The loudest thing he'd hear on an average day was a heavy cart going down cobbles, or a thunderstorm. Maybe a protest. But even that is nothing compared to the sheer sensory assault of today's London. I don't know if you've been. It's pretty relentless. Thomas Cromwell was a *very* neurotypical dude and he would have full-on sensory overload if he popped up in London today.

In any case, the most important thing for Tim was to accept that forcing his brain to do things in a way that wasn't his was not going to work. He could start to recover. There was just one problem: his sleeping. Yes, autistic people's sleeping patterns are not great at the best of times. Ask my mother, who's had to deal with mine since 1987. I just wouldn't drop off, whatever I did. How do I sleep now? Half a mirtazapine before bed at about 10 p.m. By 10:45 p.m., I'm in a coma. Yes, I do require more sleep than other people do, but nine hours of sleep a night is a price worth paying when the alternative is sleeplessness and meltdowns. Tim's problem was not that.

For some reason, Tim's body wouldn't turn off at the same time every night. If he felt sleepy at 10 p.m. on Monday, his body wouldn't let him sleep till midnight on Tuesday. The next night it'd be 2 a.m., then 4 a.m., then 6 a.m. By Saturday, his body wouldn't sleep till 8 in the morning. That means 10 hours of tossing and turning, getting increasingly frustrated with your own body, of saying, "*fuck it*", and going back to your PC to play a game. Tim's brother has the same issue, and their body clocks don't necessarily sync up – it's not like a shoe size. (My brother and I both have size 49.5 (EU)/16 (UK) shoes. Now *that's* a disability if you live anywhere outside of Holland. It was cheaper for my mum to buy three pairs of shoes and bring them to England in her hand luggage.)

This brutalising regimen, where his circadian rhythms won't sync up with the outside world, is best described as Non-24-Hour-Sleep-Wake Disorder. This is a rare condition, which is rarely diagnosed. I heard about it from watching an autistic YouTuber who suffers from it: Leslie Exp (2020). For her, it's incapacitating. She can't keep a normal job, with regular hours, because half the time she simply will not be awake. I shared what I learned with Tim. He said: "Oh shit." Throughout his life, Tim had only been told to focus on sleep hygiene – not to look at screens before bed, eat at specific times, exercise – all of that. He has yet to experiment with sleep medication, but he's nervous about its potential addictive properties. Whether that will tamp down his circadian rhythms, which are like complex jazz, is an open question. Does it have a cure? Not at the moment. But since Tim's dream is to be an independent games developer, his career choice is one of the few where he could flourish.

I speak with Tim over Discord; he usually leaves his camera off. I don't care that he does, even if it looks like I'm having a serious conversation about emotions with a cartoon panda. Sometimes, he isn't awake. Sometimes I have to wake him up. Other times, I call him and just know he needs more sleep, so we reschedule.

By the end of the year, Tim needed to retake a single module, for which he'd retake the entire year. This year saw the worst of his inertia. He didn't have any disability support besides me, an external party. It felt like the doors were shutting. Things were simply not moving. Even with body doubling, he couldn't do it. I was scared. He started trying the discipline approach again, which only made his anxiety worse. There was another period of self-isolation. In the end, I was with him when he sent off his mitigating circumstances forms and, then handed in his final coursework, which he'd put together in a massive rush.

He failed again, by a few points. Tim now had the summer to make a game from the ground up, or he'd face expulsion. I was by his side, doing extra sessions just to keep him on track. By this time, I'd joined Bridge, so I was able to discuss the situation with my boss Amanda. She saw the emails Tim got back from his university, which stated confidently that they were already providing him with all the support he needed: he had a DSA-funded autism mentor. They genuinely believed it, too. For Tim's final year, Amanda has become his study skills tutor, and I've remained his mentor.

Tim does not just meet his deadline; he does very well. For the first time since I met him, he felt joy in making games again. He is currently in his fourth year and wants to continue his education in games design. He always says he couldn't do it without me. I always tell him that he's wrong – he did all of it. What I provided was the perspective of someone who's been there, done that, and bought the T-shirt.

14
Jack

Some students don't require me to move heaven and earth for them because they already have healthy support systems. Jack is one of those students. When we started working together in October 2023, Jack's mother had been fighting my previous company because they had expected mentoring to be in place by the time his psychology degree started – an expectation that is fully justifiable. It just wasn't there. He wanted an actually autistic mentor, specifically face-to-face. I was the only one the company provided. We booked a meeting for the next day. Jack was there, with his mum and dad. We found an empty room and just chatted.

If this was an interview, I passed before I sat down. I am exactly what they wanted. It was salutary for Jack's parents to see an autistic adult who's proud of being autistic. They are both working-class, living in a small village in the countryside, a hefty drive away from the university. They hadn't seen someone be proud of their own neurotype before. I made them laugh – that helped too. Jack immediately warmed to me. It helps, too, that I'm queer; Jack is pansexual (for newbies: pansexual is not a sexual attraction to kitchenware but a capacity to be attracted to people *regardless* of that person's gender identity. To be bisexual is to be attracted to people *because* of that person's gender identity, but in different ways. My partner is bisexual and is attracted to me in a different way than he's attracted to women, for example), and he's happy to know that I know that.

I told Jack's parents about my plans to move to Bridge Mentoring. They immediately agreed. They had awful experiences with my previous company. I still get messages from mentees, all summarised as: "AAARRRGGGGH why won't **NAME OF COMPANY REDACTED** stop messaging me?!?!" The answer: late-stage capitalism. When the company replaced its customer service workers doing emails with an AI, that was the last straw. Sure, vulnerable young people will no longer have to deal with untrained people – but instead, they have to deal with a chatbot. Great. Love that for us.

We meet twice a week at Jack's university. He studies psychology, which I hold no degrees in, but, y'know, it's kind of my job now. It's not frequent that we actually talk about the degree. When he needs me, I'm there, but we often talk about different things entirely – his relationships with his parents and grandmother, his pets, his group of friends, driving (I know nothing about driving), or we simply geek out about something. He loved that I could get a pretty high score in an online game where you name the capital cities of countries and name all the world's countries on a map. I had a massive world map on my bedroom wall as a child, so I have an unfair advantage in political geography circa 1994.

Only once did Jack get angry with me. He'd been working for days on a poster presentation for a piece of group coursework, and he wanted to know whether he'd got it right. I said that nothing about the content was wrong, but I was confused about the layout. We were expected to read from top to bottom, then left to right. I told him that's not how posters usually work. Jack got very quiet for a while. I saw him scrunch his eyes together. But I stuck around, letting him blow off some steam. I ended up staying in the room for an extra two hours (I had the availability that day), and he finished the poster's layout, which was less work than he anticipated. I needed to say it. If I had avoided confrontation, he'd have been marked down for reasons that don't have anything to do with his capacities as a researcher – just for not following a structure that has arisen solely out of habitual use. He was fine with me afterwards, but I did feel nervous in the moment. Had I fucked up? I really hadn't. It was a good thing I stood my ground; Jack told me so later on.

This year is Jack's second. He's been driving to university every day on his own now. He is far more independent than before, supporting his mother when she had her operation. He's not a big reader, but he's desperate to listen to the audiobook version of this textbook, so I suppose – Hi there, Jack! You know who you are. I'll see you later in the week.

15
Emma

Emma knows what she wants. When I started working with her, I was surprised that she was able and willing to self-advocate, and if things weren't going her way, we would know about it. I didn't grow up feeling like that. When I was young, I knew I couldn't do much about how things already worked in the world. I had to adapt or crumble. Many times, though, that choice was made for me. Emma saw four different mentors before meeting me. I'm the only one who's stuck around, which is a huge compliment.

Emma studies arts practice. She's got something that I'll never have, which is fine motor skills. She's an incredible artist, making ceramics, textiles and beautiful visual work, much of it about the natural world. I am not an artist, though I have had to do a lot of art. I went to Steiner school, and I hated knitting, stitching, drawing and painting, because I was preternaturally crap at all of those. I hated working with clay because I can't stand the sensation on my hands. Art was not a safe place for me, in a way that words (and to a lesser extent music) were. But I taught English for Academic Purposes at a university specialising in the arts in 2021. Those students were all prospective artists, working on improving their English so they could travel to England in September. What I'm saying is that there is always a connection between your life and the course your students are taking.

I am not uniquely well-rounded or knowledgeable, certainly not more than any other autistic person I know.

Currently, Emma is on her professional placement. She's still making her own work, while also expanding her practice. She's learning to listen to her body, especially when it cracks and hurts. Last year, she started getting support for EDS. Ehlers-Danlos syndrome is a rare degenerative disorder, affecting the connective tissues in the body. It can cause loss of mobility and excruciating pain. Autistic people are over-represented in the cohort of people with EDS. Why? Who cares. Like with the over-representation of LGBTQIA+ autistic people vs cishet autistics, what matters is that we make autistic lives better, rather than messing around with genes that won't hold the answers anyway.

Emma teaches me that I need to be mindful of myself, too. I see Emma face-to-face since she prefers that. But I have come in to work at times when I was too burned out or ill to work. She values that but also forgives me when I get annoyed or snappy. Despite how it may seem in this book, I mess up all the time, and miscommunications between a student and me are common. As Amanda says, my main strength is my passion, but my main weakness is my passion. I care so deeply that I damage my own health to make sure I meet the needs of the students. Emma, like the others, is explicit about me taking the rest I need: "Go to bed please, Jorik." I have to. In October 2024, I got Covid twice. The second time, I was off for two weeks straight, after which I had a week's holiday in Brighton. Only then was I vaguely capable of functioning again. Emma was adamant, I needed to take this time to rest. Otherwise, I can't do my job. I relented and spent much of October curled up into a ball.

What Emma wants to do with her life is hers to decide. Currently, we're having profound conversations about artistic voice. Once, when she wasn't sure whether crochet could be included as a visual art form, I shared Björk's 2007 *Volta* photoshoots with her, and her 'Mutual Core' video from 2012. Be gay, do art, I guess. Whether she thinks she has or not, over the past several years, she has started establishing her own voice in a way that took me ten years to find. I look forward to being wowed by her in the future, too.

16 Questions and answers

1. Why are you excluding me?

Back in 2023, I got into serious trouble after going to a meeting with other mentors at one of the universities my students attend. I told them about the book you are reading right now. I believe that mentors work best from lived experience – in fact, it's the only reason I am any good at my job. It's precisely because I've experienced higher education as an autistic person that I know how to advise and support others who are currently going through it. This was, it's safe to say, not appreciated. I was the only autistic mentor of autistic students present. Others complained about me. It was a classic case of me not being comfortable in an environment not made for me. The other mentors all believed I was placing myself above them, making out that they were less capable than they were. Well, I was, and I am. To have your own, personal lived experience makes you a better mentor, especially since the relationships we have with our mentees are so, so vital. They need to know *we've* lived this too, not experienced from a distance and learned from a book; and yes, that should exclude potential mentors who are a partner, sibling or parent of an autistic person, but not themselves autistic. This book, if anything, is testament to the value of having been there and done that. If you haven't, check out question 9 instead.

2. What do I need to be able to do?

We need to learn to self-advocate, be endlessly curious, be willing to be wrong, be willing to kick up a fuss and face the consequences, be flexible for the students but inflexible on their rights, be driven by revolutionary values on a macro level and the welfare of the student on an individual one, be independent, not be an employee of the uni if you can keep that distance. In the words of Dinah Murray: be a productive irritant. Lastly: follow your heart, it guides the way.

3. Ok then – what should change?

Really? Kind of everything I suppose! Universities, we can safely assume, are not safe places for autistic people. Yes, some autistics do 'well' in the university context. Most do not, not due to lack of trying. In order to do the work we do, we have to first challenge the idea of meritocracy. Like I said, I don't believe in grades, exams or tests, for that matter. They get in the way of learning. What matters is the student's commitment to a subject of their choice. I don't believe universities are places you go to get skills for jobs. We no longer live in a world where a good education equates to a high- or even reasonably-paying job. We probably never did. Instead, I believe education to be a net good in its own right. What matters is that students find joy – genuine joy – in the work they do. They've worked incredibly hard to even get into university, let alone to survive in an environment as hostile as higher education often is. In many cases, they're already exhausted by the time they start. Some students, like Stephen, drop out before the end. That's their choice and genuinely the right thing for them. Others, like Marcus, are forced out by circumstance.

University is not a place where autistics learn to mask, in order to buy the '*opportunity*' to better oneself. At its best, it's a place where we can find our people, fuck up, fall flat on our faces, read some good books/audiobooks, engage with the wider world and build our confidence. I think it's important to make the case that education is valuable in and of itself. The better educated we are, the more likely we are to specialise in fields where our hyper-focused creativity makes us indispensable. Even then, the job market is not run for our benefit. There is a reason autistic people are the least employed subgroup of disabled people in the UK.

Universities are excellent places to learn about the world. We grow politically from connecting with people unlike us. We can find communities there. This is what universities should be for, not cram schools for training. That this is no longer the case is a detriment to the society in which we live.

4. What about your boundaries?

Why do I remain accessible to my students? Why do I care about my students in the way that I do? It's simple: because I can't not. It's why I'm good at what I do and why I go the extra mile – because it's what they would do for me in a heartbeat. That does not go one way, however. As much as I tell them to rest and be kinder to themselves, I also need to rest. The students care deeply about my wellbeing and value it more than I do. The converse is obviously also the case. Despite cultural prejudices, autistic people are great at caring about and for the wellbeing of others. Because we are taught from an early age that being uncomfortable is the price we pay to be part of society, we are pretty bad at caring for ourselves.

I still have things to learn, of course. I need others to tell me to stop working. However, from my experience, conversations about boundaries are usually used to prevent change from happening. Especially when I worked in education and the NHS, I've always been the person who takes their statutory responsibilities seriously, after which management invariably told me to be aware of my boundaries. Which is it? is the obvious question, but we're not going to focus on the inherent hypocrisies of modern managerial culture. I prefer to support someone and initiate change early so I won't have to spend weeks putting out fires, organising interruptions to study or getting people out of hospital. As the stories show, my approach is far more successful than not.

As for safeguarding, the first priority is keeping oneself and one's students safe. We need to make sure that there is someone working with you who you can confide in, who can give you advice and help you emotionally offload. We need to be mindful that our boundaries are constructs and consequences of other things we have no control over. A lot of the time, 'boundaries' are a consequence of vibes – not so much with autistic mentors, but rather with non-autistics not feeling like providing support to someone they have a duty of care over. Still, even with this knowledge, the work we do isn't boundary-less. We need to know what the limits are of what we can and should do, which differs with each mentoring relationship and changes over time. A kind of friendship will inevitably develop because of the inherent intimacy of the role. Even for students I'm exceedingly proud of – like with Adam, when he'd written a beautiful comic about being an autistic trans man – I check in before I give them a hug.

More seriously, autistic people are far more likely to be victims of sexual and relational abuse. When this book comes out, I will have started running a trial for a group for neurodivergent men with SurvivorsUK, a UK charity. No mentor should be allowed to engage in sexual or romantic relationships with their mentees. This should be a sackable offence and lead to blacklisting. Why am I so harsh? The student is in a position of vulnerability and the mentor in one of power. It is impossible to challenge that relationship, the evidence is in my case studies. The reason some relationships work and others don't is because of the implicit understanding of those rules on both sides.

Yes, to an outsider, I may seem like nothing more than a student's friend. I am equally sweary, if not more. There is a lot of laughter. We talk openly about feelings, relationships, politics, gender, sexuality, societal inequality and about fighting the powers that be. I often feel like I look a bit like the Fonz from Happy Days or Steve Buscemi in *Ghost World* – a very old, weird baby-man, hanging around the neighbourhood with children half my age. Yugh! I would respectfully disagree. So would my mentees. When it matters, I take on a different role. I have had long conversations, with Noah and Nik, say, about very profound issues they were working through, where my affect is quite different. They feel they can be vulnerable because there is nothing I can *do* with that information beyond our mentoring relationship. There is no way that I can use any of their secrets against them because I lack that power. The other reason is that, as awkward as it makes me feel to say it, I am reliable and don't fuck people about while still adhering to safeguarding regulations. If students tell me things I cannot handle alone, I report it to my supervisors. I have never had to get a student out of hospital – or committed *to* hospital – but I would in a heartbeat if necessary. What the student wants and what the student needs are paramount, though these two impulses, as stated before, are sometimes in conflict.

The trust students place in me is, however, a bit more awkward to discuss. I try not to even consider whether or not I merit their trust. I have tended to be too busy to give that part much consideration. I honestly don't think I'm doing anything inhuman, nor anything anyone else autistic wouldn't do in my place. All I have are my values; the rest is empathy, happenstance and a sense of humour. That's really it. All I have to learn now is to apply these very same processes that come naturally when advocating for others to myself. Like most autistics I know, we will die on *any* hill if we can help someone in need – just not our own.

5. Do all mentoring relationships work?

It's important to understand that not all mentoring relationships work. Our community is not a monolith, and sometimes I do fuck up. There have been three students with whom my work ended abruptly: one who couldn't handle my bad language (despite me stating I probably have Tourette's), and two due to my own fault. I had meetings with one in the early morning when I was underslept and exhausted. With the other, I, when I should have been resting, was still doing work. I overshared with one in a context where that wasn't appreciated (we both have fathers who died by suicide); with the other, I contacted their partner when they were going to drop out of university (I was in contact with their partner also, as a mentor, for a brief while). That partner was angry with me. I had a meltdown. I have had contact with neither since. These last two were the only moments where I seriously considered quitting mentoring. Why? I don't have the best self-image in the world, and criticism hits me hard, especially when I'm making myself vulnerable. It's a difficult situation to manage, but I honestly believe that they are better off working with other people.

Likewise, my line manager has told me: "your greatest strength is your passion; but your greatest weakness is also your passion." I'm not always the best person for every job. I'm a blunt instrument; I'm not subtle. If another mentor is better suited to a student, they should work with them. After a mentee hadn't shown up for a few weeks recently, I told my line manager at the mentoring company I now work for and said that I was worried the student was trying to let me down gently, thereby not using up all her hours. My line manager appreciated this greatly: she was able to reassign this student to another mentor, she is doing way, way better now. In a similar way, as an advocate, I was once invited to speak at a conference highlighting neurodivergence in the African Diaspora communities. I thanked them for the offer (which was well-paid, I hasten to add!) and contacted my friend Michael, who is a Black autistic educator himself. This time, I should not have been the only white person on the panel there. It would have been awkward, and I cannot speak to Black ND experience, nor could I claim that space. The money I would have earned would not have been justified by my own awkwardness, guilt and sense of betrayal I would have felt, even if my friends did believe I could have done some good. Michael did the event, and it went better than it could have possibly gone had I been there. Sometimes the best thing to do is to step away and let someone else do the work you shouldn't do yourself.

Students, however, are more complex. Several of my students have found it difficult, on their end, to distinguish between Jorik the mentor and Jorik as a friend. I'm not their friend, which is very difficult when their own sense of what friendships even are has been coloured by a lifetime of rejection and being let down. Marcus told me he sees me as a friend, which I've found difficult. I cannot be a friend, because friendship is based on true reciprocity. The relationships I have with students are ones that may look like a friendship to an autistic young person. They're inherently one-sided, since the attention is fully on the students, not on me. This may look like friendships they have tried to initiate with others, fully focusing their attention on their prospective friends, to the exclusion of their own needs.

Be mindful that students will want to connect. Some are lonely. Some lack other friends. The relationships that we build are complicated and, as with other education jobs, can result in students wanting to have a relationship that is more than mentorship. Romantic and sexual relations are an absolute no-no. However, when it comes to *talking* about those, a mentor absolutely should. It has been vital for my practice that I'm not shy to talk about gender, sexuality and relationships. I sometimes bring aspects of my relationship into the conversations I have with my students. I have to. My partner is really funny, which helps, and, since most of us feel subhuman in our teenage years and in our early twenties, it's humanising to be confronted with two weird queer autistics who love each other. Not all autistic people *want* relationships. Some are Ace/Aro, like Daisy. Others desperately want them but have been told their entire lives they are less than human, like Noah. Most of your students, though by no means all, will turn out to be LGBTQIA+. Sometimes they will just need to cry. And, worst of all, sometimes things just don't work out. That's okay, as painful as it is sometimes.

6. What do your students think?

Each of the students discussed in this book has been sent the story I wrote about my working relationship with them. They then gave feedback on the way their situation was represented, as well as the pseudonyms I've given them in this book. I received positive responses from all students concerned, as well as notes which I used to correct the record in accordance with their wishes. No, I will not tell you the names of individual students. If they want to share their stories, that's for them to do. I can only tell my side of things.

I have learned everything I know from the students I work with. Being a mentor is a deeply confronting job. I know I could always do better; I know I mess up way too frequently. As much as my partner likes to joke that I'm a know-it-all, I don't know what I'm doing most of the time. I'm flying blind. What I do have are my values, which lead me. I value my students' words, and I value my students' capacity to live their own lives and make their own mistakes. Sometimes these two come into conflict. The only thing to do is to discuss that conflict, with your manager, with your colleagues and, of course, with your student. Clearing the air is important. Autistic people are highly receptive to changes in emotional atmosphere. Make sure the students feel they are in control of their lives.

As stated before, I have stopped working with certain students: Daisy, Brandon and Esther all graduated in 2024; Marcus decided to leave education. I've stopped seeing other students for different reasons. Sometimes, the student decides to no longer meet with me or any other mentor. When I feel like a student isn't happy, I check in with them to see if they'd prefer to work with someone they do gel with. On two occasions, which I mentioned in a previous answer, the student and I stopped working together in a less-than-pleasant way. That will also happen. The most important thing after a setback is to get back up again, dust yourself off and continue, wiser and more capable. I'm not saying *'don't feel pain'* when you – you *as a person* – are rejected like that. *Do* feel it. Work through it, using self-compassion. Be empathetic towards yourself. As my friends never tire of telling me, I'm a flagrant hypocrite when it comes to who I show empathy to (spoilers: it ain't me, babe). If a student isn't able (it's rare they aren't willing) to be empathetic towards you as a fellow autistic, then that's okay too. Work through it. You'll come out of it stronger. No one has a clean slate when it comes to being a mentor. Thank goodness this job isn't done via an app, where one bad faith negative review will have serious consequences for your earning capacity.

All the students present have stated and restated their commitment to this book, this story and the work that I have done/do with them. Lissa told me, remember, it's not my fault that places be ableist (for my editor: the use of the copula 'be' instead of a conjugation is Gen Z internet lingo. Lissa uses it because she's young and cool and such). In the end, like Esther, they may all one day want to become their own Adam, or Lissa, or Emma or Nik. They can only be the best mentors *they* can be because *they* are autistic, in their own unique way.

7. How do I stop myself from burning out?

When I signed the contract for this book, my intentions were to show how valuable it is to be a lone autistic voice in the neurotypical world of higher education. But after the 2023 mentors' meeting, I was not allowed to return to that university because of my use of language and how it made people "*uncomfortable*". My previous mentoring company was unwilling to stand up for me, even stating that the university had some good points to make. I needed to know my limits. As you know from what I've written before, I will self-flagellate when I'm criticised like that.

At the time of the call, I'd been speaking to my friend Joe, who I co-run the AutWell group with, at a local café. I was a bit teary by the end."Not good?" he asked. "Not good", I said. Not good at all.

A few weeks later, I put together a poster of sorts for this very book, highlighting the necessity of lived experience of neurodivergence for this job. I went to an autism conference in Bristol, where the poster would be shown. I saw a few familiar faces; I met a lot more who weren't. It was a great experience. The final speaker was a mentor himself who, it turns out, approached his practice in the exact same way I was doing. He was funny, a charming shambles, his full attention directed at the student's health and wellbeing, not the university's. He opened the floor for questions.

> "Hi I'm Jorik, and I am also a mentor. I do the exact same thing you do, but I just got a massive slap on the wrist from the company I work for. How do you do what we do and not get in trouble?"
>
> "Er – don't get caught!"

We got in touch later on. His name is Brian Irvine, a neurodivergent mentor, who works at UCL, the place where a previous mentor told me that things "must be so hard for you." He will be one of the first people to read this full manuscript.

What we focused on was whether or not we, as mentors, need to have walked the walk as well as talked the talk. Brian is not autistic, in his words, though he does have aphantasia. For me, the distinction is irrelevant – what diagnosis you do or do not have. You are a way better mentor for autistic students if you are yourself autistic, no matter what name or diagnostic label you feel like sticking to. Brian, I told him, is one of us, which expresses the connection better than anything seen through a neurotypical deficit lens.

Brian believes it can and should be possible to work within a system, even when that system intends to get rid of us. I'm not so sure that I can. I'm too annoying. I don't work well within large organisations. I need to have the independence to be an activist, to be an arsehole. For one student – let's call him Victor – the invitation for a workshop on ABA was a step too far. He organised within the student union and called for a boycott of this external company. I did not have any input in that decision. He made that decision himself, and he takes the credit for stepping up. What I did share was my own perspective on ABA and the views within the disability rights community. The meeting was first moved online, then cancelled altogether, due to lack of interest from the student body. If I had been attached to the university, I would have been reprimanded – or worse – for claiming that anything the university did or said was ableist or unethical. Not because they would be right, but because my contract would highlight my responsibility towards my employer over and above my ethical considerations about the work that they do.

That is not to call out any specific university in particular, just to state that there are very serious consequences for whistleblowers and people who call out unethical practices in the workplace. It's far easier to just go with the flow. But I'm the kind of person who cannot help but step up. I cannot handle being in a position where I have to be ethically compromised to do my job. I'm certainly not alone in that. Other people are less black and white than I am. I applaud that, and I hope they succeed in breaking through barriers from within a system rather than without. I'm just saying that I can't, for very personal reasons. If you want to be a mentor, then that is a decision you will have to make for yourself. Try it out, see what fits best. But as for me, I far prefer making trouble from just outside the institution.

Brian, most helpfully of all, gave me the details of a company owned and run wholly by neurodivergent people, with a wholly autistic leadership team. This is Bridge Mentoring, who I am definitely plugging here, despite potential charges of conflict of interest. Yes, I *do* have an interest in seeing Bridge succeed. I succeed when they do, and vice versa. I interviewed with them, passing the interview pretty much within seconds, because they could see what I did aligned with their values. Brian's recommendation helped too.

At my previous company, I no longer felt comfortable relaying students' distress to their staff. According to them, not one member of staff had had autism training. When I proposed that I could provide it, I was fobbed off. When, in November 2021, I called the company several times to express concerns that other students had raised with me – particularly regarding ableist and queerphobic attitudes expressed by staff and other mentors – I was told to no longer call, due to me "upsetting members of staff." It wasn't what I said that they had issues with, just the seriousness with which I stated my concerns – staff had no training to deal with autistic people. Additionally, none of my concerns about ableism, queerphobia or the content of the training modules were engaged with seriously. The manager asked if I was feeling mentally well. Okay, wow. That sounds pretty similar to what happened to me at drama school – it's not my actions that are the problem, it's me doing those actions. When I responded that I no longer felt confident that complaints would be taken seriously because I am myself autistic, the same manager said: "Oh, we don't want you to feel unwelcome!"

I stayed at the company for another 18 months before deciding to leave. But when I did, I couldn't have chosen a worse time to do so. The Student Loans Company in England was going through a restructuring, where they would stop working with external needs assessment agencies. If my students wanted to move with me, they needed their needs assessors to sign off on the change. Most needs assessors my students had worked with had gone out of business by the end of 2023. Additionally, they were unbearably slow at booking meetings for students who had not yet had their DSA sorted before they began their degrees. It took 10 months for all the students who could, to move, in dribs and drabs. Ten months. It was horrendous. There were periods in between where I was barely paid due to the delays caused by the SLC's changes in policy. With some students, I have had to give up being paid for the work I'd done. The SLC simply refused to pay me, despite Bridge and I doing everything we could. My lesson: despite there being an explicit need and a duty of care, the institution responsible for the delays was unwilling to pay me for the work I'd done.

You are worth something. You are worth being paid. This is, after all, your job. I would have never allowed anyone else to work tonnes of hours without pay. This is the so-called passion tax, also referred to as enthusiasm exploitation. When we work in fields that are important to us, doing work we care about, that opens us up to exploitation. Businesses and organisations love staff who go above and beyond, so they don't have to pay us for all the extra value that we bring. It's easier for them to quietly accept that we're responsible people who care about our work and count their money. But, if we continue going above and beyond, we *will* burn out. I did. Hard.

In early 2024, I had a meeting with a member of staff at Wired Differently to ascertain how the UK government, through a benefit called Access to Work, would be able to help me. Question one: how many hours did I work each week? Well, I'd just stopped teaching languages alongside the mentoring, mostly in the evenings and weekends. I was winding down my tutoring work as well, teaching English to students via the National Tutoring

Programme, aimed at supporting students who'd missed education during the Covid-19 pandemic. I thought I was doing okay: "Well, if we're looking at contact hours, that's about… 41 hours a week." Her: "What about emails?" Long pause. "…65?" She immediately said: "more like 80." That was true. At the time, my partner was not working, recovering from physical injuries and a depressive episode, so I also took responsibility for keeping the house vaguely passable, as well as shopping, admin, cooking, making sure we had clean clothes, etc. I basically only worked or slept. If I was going to carry on like this, I would die. I told Amanda about this. She understood. She spent hours and hours trying to get all the students I was seeing moved over to Bridge Mentoring in the face of institutional inertia. She saw I wasn't coping.

In 2024, I spent more time than I ever had done recovering. It was tough. My patience for myself was limited. When I did have meetings with my students, they would often reiterate how necessary it was for me to rest more and work less. So did Amanda. When we got to August, she told me that, for some students, the mentoring I provided would never be funded by DSA. I was distraught: that was about £6,000, for work I'd done and would never be paid for. Is this work worth it if I don't get paid for it? Yes, but then it's volunteering, requiring a totally different relationship with the student. Working as a mentor without being paid for your labour and experience is exploitative, especially if a multinational company is hoovering up the profits. I keep returning to money, though, not because I'm obsessed, but because it's highly necessary to approach this relationship in a professional, not personal, capacity. This is what distinguishes the relationship between mentor and mentee. This is how we enforce the kind of friendship we develop and distinguish it from a reciprocal relationship. When mutual, reciprocal responsibilities come into the picture, that means we can no longer be a mentor and a mentee. The one-sided focus of the mentor-mentee relationship is vital: it allows us to be committed to the student. My experience with Daisy is an example of when that doesn't work. The basis of our relationship *must* be unequal. The kind of friendship I'm talking about is complex and will have to be hammered out between the mentor and mentee. But it must always be centred on the mentee, with the mentor opening up to the benefit of the mentee. Sometimes, it *is* important to reiterate that disconnect. The mentor will be an important part of the student's life, as per the wishes of that student, not the other way around. If the student chooses and re-chooses to work with a mentor, then the mentor's time will be a vital one in the life of the mentee. But the mentor themselves? They get paid. It's our job. At a certain point, we have to refuel, recover. I was fortunate enough to already have a community of autistic queers around me who I could confide in. Not everyone is so lucky. If you over-commit to your mentees, you will burn out. If you are unable to dislodge yourself from mentees should they choose to move on, you may feel resentment. That is not a sin in itself, but make sure that you don't start expecting a reciprocal check-up from your mentees. That's not what this relationship is supposed to be about.

8. How do I make communities with other mentors?

Whether you are within an already existing organisation or not, it is vital that you are not alone in your work. I really suffered from not being around others for years, who I knew had the best interests of myself and my students at heart. The company just wanted to make money. Instead, through my work, I met other mentors. With some – neurotypical – the communication was awkward, see my experience in mid-2023. But with other actually autistic mentors, the experience has been enormously gratifying. Working with Bridge Mentoring has been even better. I feel supported in a way I never was at my previous company. Sometimes, it's necessary to vent with someone. Nearly all students I have worked with hit points where they were in a state where I was concerned for their health. Some, like Nik, were just coming out of a very tricky period when we started working together. Therapists have therapists. And while what we do is more practical than therapy, we still need people to support us. In my previous employment, I was not confident that the staff knew how to deal with students in a bad state. According to their own statements, the company's staff was never trained on autism, beyond having to take the internal training modules I have written about previously, which only a small minority of staff took. That is all fine now, I have heard the company replaced most of its staff with a generative AI system (read: an algorithm focused on maximising profit) with a chatbot and an automated messaging service. I did not feel safe to discuss my work with *any* of those people, so I didn't. I was my own safeguarding system. That, in the end, started wearing me down. I needed to work with other people in order for me not to be the person responsible for all the students' pain. It's difficult not to let it affect you, either. When students are upset, their pain leaks into me, even over Zoom or Google Meet. That is because we are both autistic and because in many cases I've been in exactly the same amount of mental and emotional pain. My partner is a teaching assistant for autistic children, a job he started in early 2024. Despite how much joy it gives him, being around young people in states of distress, overload and meltdown is draining, emotionally. Because autistic people, especially if we're tired, can easily feel the emotions of others around us, sometimes confusing them with our own. Distinguishing between our emotions and the ones from the people and animals in our vicinity can be an exhausting part of our day. Having to provide support to these young people, in pain, hurts us. This is called emotional contagion, though I prefer the term emotional porousness, since contagion has a very negative ring. Added to the difficulties autistics face in even figuring out what our *own* emotions are when we're so busy processing the outside world on a second-by-second basis – alexithymia – we are often really tired indeed, which goes right back into the vicious cycle of greater porousness, and greater distress and greater exhaustion. That way lies burnout.

Any line manager understands that our empathy is the centre of our power, at the very basis of what makes autistic people good at their jobs. Therefore, it's important for supervisors and managers to have as proactive an attitude to employee welfare as mentors have to their students. There will have to be moments when you as a line manager step in and not let your staff burn out. Creating communities is a vital part of that, though this should be done in a non-intrusive and validating way. When multiple autistic staff members are working in a neurotypical environment (read: every *single* environment known to man, with the potential absence of one's own room, or in our chosen families), the expectations we are faced with are massive. The complications we face having to unmask in environments where masking is our main protection against harm are not ones we can face alone. This is where we need check-ins, places to exchange war stories, knowing there's someone, or a series of someones, who have your back. My partner and I do that for one another and we're very good at it. Not everyone has that safety net. Make sure you build yours. Line managers: make sure you have the capacity to support your staff, as we support our students. Yes, the initial cost to your time and capacity may be higher, but even from an amoral, financial perspective, not having burned-out staff helps an awful lot. When we are not burned out, we can actually provide the services that can save lives, validate students and give them the support they deserve. Who knows, those students might one day want to join as mentors too.

9. I'm neurotypical. How can I help?

We cannot do this work without you – your commitment to our cause is vital. But the most important thing for you is, for the moment, to not centre the conversation around yourselves. The neurodiversity movement is young and still fragile. We can learn from previous organising in anti-racist, feminist, environmental, disability and anti-capitalist movements. I don't think sharing and reposting on social media is enough, or even all that helpful. The algorithm isn't interested in liberation, only in driving us further towards cishet white male patriarchy and a furthering of the capitalist hellhole we have the misfortune to call home. When you do not share our particular intersection and existence, maybe allowing us to speak for ourselves is the best thing to do. In the meantime, check for yourself: why are you interested in supporting autistic people? Do you feel you have something to teach us about how to be a human being, like you? Thanks but no thanks. Instead, if you feel a connection to us, an empathetic link, rather than just something to be fixed, check in with yourself. Maybe you're not as neurotypical as you thought you were.

10. Where do you see this field in ten years?

This is going to hurt, perhaps, but right now, I don't see an immediate solution to the access problems faced by neurodivergent students in higher education, let alone in wider society. These issues are endemic. Even at the time of writing, in late 2024, yet another BBC exposé of special needs-provision finds abuse of autistic children. Yes, of course. Because the world as it is right now *is* abusive to autistic people. Because the people charged with caring for them do the exact opposite, simply by adhering to the systems they'd been taught. This is not a case of abuse being abhorrent to the system, it *is* the system. We treat autistic children and adults like human waste and are surprised that this is contrary to human rights. The mainstream conversation about autism is a needle that's fundamentally impossible to thread because of a lack of understanding of us as humans and of what their own preconceptions about us mean for their own behaviour. What we as actually autistic people need to do is gather together, build our own strength and stop arguing for others to accept us as human. They have no reason to, just yet. You can't bring social change by sheer force of will. There need to be serious changes to capitalist society in order for autistic people's humanity to be understood. I was once asked by a charity fighting homelessness: how do we stop autistic people becoming homeless? My answer was simple: "free housing, free and accessible education, healthcare and social care and a universal basic income that meets everyone's needs." That's not something a single charity can easily do. In order for autistic people to have an equal shot at existing, we need radical societal change towards a change in ownership of the means of production. Representation does not equal equity. The richest man alive right now is diagnosed autistic. That hasn't – and won't – make any one of my students' lives any better, probably significantly worse.

Instead, what we can do is provide a safe haven. Recognise that we as autistic people are square pegs in the round hole of higher education. Verbalise that. Like them, you have also struggled in your higher education. Your struggles are not the same, especially if you are not yourself queer, say, or from a non-white background. We have fights on our hands, so it's vital that we have a place to be safe and fight for it, like Lissa did for hers.

11. Ok, could you, like, systematise this?

As you can see from even the small sample of students I've worked with as an autistic mentor, all chose degrees that were different. I could talk more easily about creative writing than I could about physics, sure, but being autistic, there are few fields in which I could not connect my own previous reading, interests and fascinations. I loved having Brandon explain complex maths to me, even if I struggled to understand some of it.

I'm not a games designer, like Marcus, but I love video games and am aware of issues in the industry. Unlike Lissa, I am not a classicist, but I've read up on the subject while doing research for my own work. I'm not a biologist, but I shared Daisy's joy when she talked about bacterial genera that were barely studied. I am not an engineer at all, but Nik and I researching recent Indian economic history together was a blast for both of us. Yes, I have done an English degree, but my interests are far wider than that. My first piece of advice: be interested in everything. Allow your natural autistic joy to be the first thing you communicate. That's where the student and you will connect first.

As every country, city, university, course, major, minor and student are different, I can't proclaim a single system to be inviolably right at all times. Instead, I am very happy to work with the institutions you work for and the companies that provide mentoring to lay out systems, appropriate to your contexts. However, I do have some ground rules.

I. Be yourself.
II. Say that you will unmask and then actually do so, if your student allows that too – which they might not, at least not at first.
III. Be willing to challenge the student when they are acting against their own best interests. They deserve the best, even if they don't believe they do.
IV. Always value the student's safety over and above your job security. You will likely anyway, because you're autistic.
V. Break toxic, ableist narratives around 'boundaries' and instead create your own, mutually constructed relationship

with mentees, though with the caveat that *you* are the mentor and *they* the mentee.

VI. Never take advantage of a student's feelings towards you. They are not your friend. You, instead, are supporting them.

VII. Find support from colleagues and professionals, as well as close autistic friends, *never* from mentees.

VIII. Be willing to fight the system. Our existence is already threatened by being in the world, so we might as well try to change it.

12. How can we find you? (my details)

https://www.jorikmol.com

Conclusion

This book's stories will help you, I hope, to see the job we do as more than a paycheck. You have huge responsibilities. As Marcus said, I helped him "learn to *be* autistic". Be an advocate. Use your autistic curiosity and share what gives you joy. Not in a patronising way – but in a way that is real, genuine. Autistic people have to mask all day. Being autistic is exhausting. But every story I tell in this book is representative because autistic people are as diverse as everyone else.

The *kind of friendship* I describe appearing with all my students is, I think, the most complicated concept I've addressed. I am committed to the welfare of the student. Despite sometimes calling them "bro", "dude" or "kiddo" when I'm really proud of them, I cannot be a *real* friend. The relationship is too skewed. This is tough for people who aren't comfortable unmasking in front of the students, but it does require a sense of stability in one's own self. For someone with abusive tendencies, not just abusive education (such as ABA-training), but potential for emotional, physical, even sexual abuse are rife. It is vital that mentors face rigorous checks before starting to work with students, as well as get support from other mentors and managers in order to do their job properly. My advice: work independently from a large institution, like a university. As someone working for an independent contractor, you have the freedom to challenge the university's policies. As a mentor, you are committed to the welfare of the students, not the continued existence of the university. That may sound like common sense, but if you're autistic, you are very likely to have been pushed out of a job because you stood up for something you believed in. All of my autistic friends have had problematic experiences in the workplace because we speak out on behalf of people we are expected to protect. When the protection instinct goes up against the practical considerations of functioning in a modern company or institution, we are far more likely to choose what we believe to be ethically right. This means that autistic workers have a tendency to be seen as holier-than-thou, which is a bit rich, since the reason we're standing up for the safety of others should be the *baseline* expectation.

A few years ago, my friend was pushed out of a job she loved because she valued the safety and wellbeing of students over and above the reputation of the educational institution she worked for. Of course, these cases will never go to court; of course, we would never win if they did. There is a level of inbuilt, logical selfishness within larger organisations that allows them to survive in capitalist contexts. Staff internalise those values and end up choosing to keep schtum when misdeeds, violence and/or abuse take place where they work. Rather than highlighting the necessity of speaking out against injustice, in order to keep good relationships with staff, we don't speak out.

From this book, you should have a clear understanding of what it is I do. I connect with every student. Sometimes this works well; at other times, it doesn't. I have even shared examples of things going badly wrong. The fact is that we, as mentors, have a difficult but incredibly rewarding job. We have a unique responsibility, which allows us to make a difference in the face of systems that seem built to destroy us. We can, actually, do better. As mentors, we can and should put our politics into practice. Higher education can and should be better. Let's do something that breaks the rules. We need to. Our community needs it. We need you. Let's break those boundaries, together.

Recommended projects/ assignments/ discussion questions

1. Set up an autistic-only environment, in the style of Jorik's *AutWell* Group, to allow autistic students to find a safe space to unmask.
2. Create an Autistic Pride Day, preferably not in April.
3. Reflect on the distinction between what mentors with lived experience can bring to mentees, versus mentors without.
4. If you are autistic and hiding it, find spaces to come out as yourself and find the community you've deserved all these years.
5. Should you decide to use this book in your own practice as a mentor or educator, write about your experiences and get in touch. I'd love to hear from you.

References

Kupferstein, H. (2018). Evidence of increased PTSD symptoms in autistics exposed to applied behavior analysis. *Advances in Autism*, 4(1), 19–29. https://doi.org/10.1108/AIA-08-2017-0016

Leslie Exp (2020). *Non-24 Hour Sleep-Wake Disorder: My Experience – YouTube.* 24 November 2020. Available at: https://www.youtube.com/watch?v=Cl8_pkND1DU (Accessed: 22 December 2024).

Milton, D. E. M. (2012). On the ontological status of autism: the 'double empathy problem'. *Disability & Society*, 27(6), 883–887. https://doi.org/10.1080/09687599.2012.710008

Sasson, N. J., Faso, D. J., Nugent, J., Lovell, S., Kennedy, D. P., Grossman, R. B. (2017). Neurotypical peers are less willing to interact with those with autism based on thin slice judgments. *Scientific Reports*, 7, 40700. doi: 10.1038/srep40700. PMID: 28145411; PMCID: PMC5286449.

Srinivasan, A. (2022) *The Right to Sex*. London: Bloomsbury.

Thomas, I. (2018). Asperger's Children by Edith Sheffer review – the origins of autism in Nazi Vienna. The Guardian [online]. Available at: https://www.theguardian.com/books/2018/jul/27/aspergers-children-origins-autism-nazi-vienna-edith-sheffer-review (Accessed: 5 February 2025).

Wynn, N. (2018). *Incels | ContraPoints*. – YouTube. 17 August 2018. Available at: https://www.youtube.com/watch?v=fD2briZ6fB0 (Accessed: 22 December 2024).

Recommended further reading

Mol, J. (2026). *Feeling Fast and Slow*. London: Hachette.

Rothwell, J. (Director). (2021). *The Reason I Jump* [Film].

Silberman, S. (2015). *Neurotribes: The Legacy of Autism and the Future of Neurodiversity*. New York: Avery.

Index

ABA [and "conversion therapy"] viii, 1–2, 7, 9, 12, 41–42, 85, 97–99, 140, 153

Adam and Gender Identity 17–27

ADHD vii, 115–116

alexithymia 31, 66–67, 94–95, 112, 147

anxiety 34, 67, 73–74, 92–94, 119. See also: OCD

Asperger's Syndrome 5–6

Asperger, Hans 5–6

Attwood, Tony xiv

autistic inertia 109, 115–119

AutWell (Autistic Wellbeing Group, run by Jorik at Bath Spa University) xii, 25, 26, 27, 30, 107, 139, 156

BDSM/kink 112

body doubling p. 119

Brandon and Conversion therapy 39–43

burnout 40, 64, 147

consent 111–113

Daisy and Boundaries 69–80

Disability in different countries 84–86

Disability/Disabled vii–viii, xvi, 2–3, 21, 37, 40, 52, 55, 59, 60, 82–83

Emma and Self-Advocacy 125–127

Esther and Alexithymia 61–68

Friendship xv, 13, 32, 42, 43, 76–80, 103, 132–133, 136, 145, 152, 153

hyperfocus xv, 105, 115, 131

incels 51–53, 109–111

Jack and Family 121–123

Kupferstein, Henny 41

Lissa and Systems of Power 49–60

Marcus and Class 29–38

masturbation 104, 110–111

meltdowns xiv, xv, 11, 13, 30, 77, 93, 94, 135, 147

Miles and Self-destruction 45–47

Milton, Damian vii, 6, 12, 74

Minchin, Jo 2

neurochauvinism vii, 7, 16, 50

Neuroqueer xii, 1, 7

Nik and External Stressors 101–107

Noah and Sexuality 109–113

OCD 116–117

orientalism viii

person-first language 8–9

race/racism vii, 8–9, 10, 49, 52, 101–102, 135–136, 148, 150

Said, Edward vii

Scheffer, Edith 5–6

Stephen and Self-medication 91–100

stimming xv, 42, 112

substance use 65, 92–93, 96

Tim and Medical Obstacles 115–120

Walker, Nick viii, 2, 7

Zoey and the Social Model of Disability 81–89

www.ingramcontent.com/pod-product-compliance
Lightning Source LLC
Chambersburg PA
CBHW070807230426
43665CB00017B/2519